To Bill —
Thank you
of support and encouragement.
YBIC, Jay

Men and the Church:
Is there a Future?

by

Jay Crouse

Foreword by Dr. Hayes Wicker

Note to the Reader: The anecdotal illustrations in this book are true to life, based on my experience with ministry to men. Real men's identities are disguised. When I name specific men with last names, I've received the permission of the men involved. All other characters and stories involve composites of real guys and situations encountered in my ministry and any resemblance to people living or dead is coincidental.

Cover Design by Notion Design Group
Cover photograph by Barbara Banks
Olympic torch photograph by Maria Lyle
Part III photograph by Barbara Banks
Back cover photograph by Hal Stephan
All other photographs by the author

www.xulonpress.com

Dedication

For my beloved sons
John, Philip, Edward and William,
the most important, godly men in my life.

Contents

PART 3: A BLESSED HOPE
The Churched Man

He will be blessed, if he learns to follow his Lord. . .

Introduction

I don't know which movie he said it in, but the statement is forever identified with the Duke. Of course, I'm speaking of John Wayne, for years the symbol of the American West and manly men and his motto: "A man's gotta do what a man's gotta do." He's the same guy who also spoke of "Being scared to death, but saddling up anyway." Good advice.

Circle the wagons because manhood is under attack in America. At the very least, it is either misunderstood or maligned. Most guys are neither Macho Man nor Nacho Man, neither an iron man nor a couch potato. However, many have grown up with the model of being a Disney-fied Prince Charming or a sissified "girly man". Now even super heroes are depicted as those with serious flaws, fears, baggage and self-doubt. The Man of Steel is a bundle of contradictions. Batman needs to get out of the cave more often and stay away from the Bat-mobile. Ironman is Neurosis Man.

As a pastor for over 42 years in a local church and over 21 years at the same church, I have long had a passion for discipling men. We structured our Wednesday night program many years ago around Refresher Women's Ministry and Band of Brothers. We guys intentionally schedule times to lift up, listen up, huddle up and then man up.

The inescapable fact is that men need a *Paul* to mentor them, a *Timothy* to disciple and a *Barnabas* as a close, Christian friend who will be with them in the trenches of the battle for godliness. Author and men's ministry leader Jay Crouse has exemplified all three of these key roles. I have watched over the years how the Lord has raised him up to a key position of leadership in his denomination. As a pace-setting innovator and now as a groundbreaking author, he is calling men of all denominations to be difference-makers in a man-culture of community and ministry.

Jay particularly hones in on the defection and alienation of men from the church. Admittedly, I am over 40 and did not grow up in a digital world. Multi-tasking is something my kids do. However, the future of the church and the nation is in reaching the current generation of post-Christian young men, moving them from the subversion of the world to transformation in Christ. Of course, the middle-aged and older guys are also desperately needy of the Good News.

While that wonderful term for abiding in the Vine – "in Christ" – is used about 90 times in the New Testament, scripture calls us to develop a specific game plan for how the branches can bear fruit. He uses Holy Spirit leadership and teaching to flesh out the practicality of reaching those with a hole-in-the-soul that only Christ can fill.

We men love stats—batting averages, free throw percentages, golf handicaps, fairway-to-greens-in regulation, etc. Jay backs up the seriousness of our spiritual challenge with eye-popping statistics. I gulped more than once and then I was convicted of my own personal lack of empathy for the unchurched. However, I was also challenged to strategize more effectively.

I wish that I had his book as a resource years ago and particularly when we started our local Men's Ministry. I did not know of any other church that had wholly dedicated Wednesday worship and/or prayer time to unique, specific men's and women's ministries. Jay Crouse provides help galore for each of us in different denominations to develop our own strategies, which will allow for the discipling of men, resulting in better husbands, fathers and servants of the Master.

As we men get older, we long to be true heroes to our children and grandchildren and to leave a lasting legacy. The toys that served as status symbols and the portfolios that seem to provide security no longer matter so much. This book will remind us once again that only two things last forever—the Word of God and people.

The Lord, through the author, will convict you as I have been for the need of a BHAJ (Big Holy Audacious Journey). After all, as Augustine noted centuries ago, "Our hearts are restless till they find rest in God." You have a coach in Crouse.

This book actually gives the "how to" of developing comprehensive men's ministry in any kind of church. Each chapter provides next step action plans, personal reflection questions and group discussion. The listing of bibliographies, studies, surveys and practical tips is comprehensive. Whether you are a pastor or a layman, you will benefit from these timely tips and insights. They are gleaned not from software or a classroom, but from the laboratories of love in the home and in the church. Jay is a practitioner, not a researcher.

Let me add a word of explanation. Jay's present ministry and background is in a liturgical, mainline church. The terms and concepts will be foreign to those of us in some fundamental or evangelical circles. He certainly believes in salvation by grace through faith. Some readers might find it too mystical or formal in terms of application, but the differences in denominational approaches are presented. However, Christians in America have been blessed by the writings of Anglicans such as C. S. Lewis and John Stott. As high impact players with intellectual and spiritual heft, they have stretched our thinking.

As the pastor of Chuck Colson for over 20 years, I was privileged to lead a memorial service for him in our First Baptist Church of Naples, Florida and then to participate in an ecumenical funeral service in the National Cathedral. Yes, I was out of my comfort zone. Big time. Rejoice when others love Jesus in a different manner (1 Corinthians 12:12; 14:20). We all play different instruments in the band, but hopefully harmonize with each other and with the score of scripture. I urge you to "receive" Jay Crouse, "a choice man in the Lord" (Romans 16:13). May every man who is *in* the Lord be *for* his brothers.

This book is a trumpet call for us to be on the offensive, since Jesus promised that "the gates of Hades would not prevail against" us (Matthew 16:18). That means that Satan and his dominion with its philosophies are on the defense behind the gates. We are not cowering behind our walls waiving a white flag of surrender. Nor are we like the defenders of the Alamo who were told to stand firm, but not to expect reinforcements. Read this book and find hope, help and honor in a mission possible. We will truly say, "No man left behind."

Dr. Hayes Wicker
Senior Pastor
First Baptist Church Naples, Florida

Preface

Whether in gatherings or in solitary reflection, there is a hunger on the part of men to understand the potential of their masculine spirit.
                                              -**David James**[1]

Isn't it great to be a man?
We can open our own jars.
We are guilt-free as we walk out of a motel room - without making the bed.
We're able to pick our teeth with any sharp object.
We can do all of our Christmas shopping in one day.
We can excuse ourselves from the table and visit the restroom . . . alone.

And long before John Gray wrote his book, we knew that women are from Venus, and we are from Mars.[2] However, as great as it is to be a man, we face significant challenges. An overview of men in America today indicates that:

- *We are friendless.*
- *We have allowed ourselves to become emotionally isolated.*

- *We are confused about what makes for an authentic man and what men's roles are.*
- *We are success driven; and some feel that we're prone to success-sickness.*
- *We are spiritually seeking.*[3]

Unfortunately, although we are spiritually seeking, we've been avoiding church attendance in droves since the 1960s. A national survey on church attendance by the US Congregational Life Survey revealed that there are more women (61%) than men (39%) in our church pews.[4] Data from a variety of national research groups put American men's church attendance at between 32% to 35% of our general population. Historical data resources reveal that in the 1950s men's church attendance was over 50%. The bottom line for us as church leaders and emerging leaders, is that we face a spiritual crisis with men in this country.

Why aren't men attending church? Through the perspective of twenty-five years of ministering in the mission field of American men, I have come to the sad conclusion that men do not see value in church-life in the church of Jesus Christ.

Don't see value in the sacred institution that embodies the transformational, life-giving word and sacraments of Jesus Christ and which, at its core, is intended to satisfy those who are spiritually seeking? How is that possible?

Clearly, we church leaders have neglected our men here—not meanly, not intentionally, and not even in our conscious awareness. We've done it through *benign neglect.*

BENIGN NEGLECT
Noun. **an attitude or policy of ignoring an often delicate or undesirable situation that one is held to be responsible for dealing with.**

That's the Merriam-Webster definition of our core problem—ignoring a situation instead of assuming our legitimate responsibility for improving it.[5] If there is to be a future for men and the church, benign neglect has got to go. That is the theme of this book and the reason for the prescriptions it offers. Is there a future for men and the church? By no means is the outlook certain. We might continue with benign neglect. We might fail. And that possibility haunts me, because the potential for the churched man is so filled with joy. But we've got hard work to do, especially in our mainline denominational churches. In fact, it's a battle. And the battle is mostly uphill.

Several leading men's ministry writers have made the point, time and again, that the bigger the man shortage in a church, the more likely that church is going *downhill*, in numbers and community influence. As we prepare to thoughtfully and intentionally consider the future of men in our denominational churches, let me offer data from my own denomination, the Episcopal Church. I shudder at statistics like the following:

- **Episcopalians have the largest "gender gap"—the ratio of men to women—of any mainline denomination with a 12 percent difference.[6]**
- **From the year 1915 to 2011, we went from 8,506 parishes to 6,736.**
- **From the year 1965 to 2011, we went from 3,615,643 baptized members to 1,923,046 (and the 1990s was the "Decade of Evangelism" for us!)**
- **From the year 2002 to 2011, the national average Sunday attendance dropped from 846,640 to 657,887.[7]**

I've volunteered to be part of the needed turnaround. In 1999, after twenty-five years of working in the private sector,

I became a full-time lay minister serving Episcopal Bishop John Lipscomb in the Diocese of Southwest Florida as the first Director of Episcopal Men's Ministries. This regional denominational ministry to men emerged in leading an ecumenical ministry known as A Journey in Disciple Making. We provided this unique resource for men, seeking to intentionally equip men as disciple makers in their local churches.

What a joy it was to see men boldly stepping forward to be equipped and sent! These were men of all ages, as a band of brothers, committed to taking southwest Florida for Jesus Christ.

A few years ago, I moved forward from my diocesan duties to launch the ministry of Men and the Church. But I am no lone ranger. In my many years in ministry to men, I stand on the shoulders of, and walk arm in arm with, many men's ministry leaders and friends—beginning with my dad, who instilled in me a passion for my faith. I am also greatly indebted to Bill McCartney, Dale Schlafer, and the mighty work of Promise Keepers in the 1990s. And I owe much to former Bishop John Lipscomb, Pat Morley, David Delk, Dan Erickson, Robert Lewis, Bob Hamrin, Ron Doyle, Hal Haddan, Father Andrew Mayes, and hundreds of Christian men in southwest Florida.

Carrying a passion for men's ministry up and down the Florida coast, with a terrific team of pastors and volunteers, I have seen some remarkable results. We've hosted regional, county, and local church conferences, seminars, and workshops. We have implemented local church ministry programs in over 50 of our 78 Episcopal churches in the Southwest Florida Diocese. We created and led a unique ecumenical initiative entitled "Equipping the 70" in which over 125 Christian men were equipped to disciple 1000 new men of faith. And most recently our initiative, Behold the Man, annually leads men on their pilgrimage to the Holy Land.

Such forays in the battle to conquer our "man crisis" have been my passion for decades now. From the brutal statistics emerged a vision—from a bishop and a lay leader—a big, holy, and audacious goal: *to reach men in the way Jesus reached them.*

How Did Jesus Draw Men into His Church?

- He **called them** (Mark 1:16-20). The fact is, 95 percent of Christian men have responded to this call and are in our local churches. They are the ones we need to equip, through a dynamic model, to welcome men back to church.
- He **trained them** with a perfect model to prepare them for a huge adventure (Luke 10:1-20). The "sending of the seventy" describes Jesus' model: He mentored, equipped, sent, brought back, mentored, equipped, etc.
- He **poured into them** His life—into twelve men using His model. For three years they watched, listened, and imitated their Master and mentor.
- He **sent them** on a big adventure to transform the world (Matthew 28:19-20). He was sending competent, equipped disciples to make more disciples.

Again, sadly, for men at least, the church has mostly forgotten what Jesus intended to happen to men through His church: that we become equipped *to go.* That model for equipping disciple makers, created two thousand years ago, has in most churches *disappeared!*

So, I say again, this battle is uphill. Please join me in advancing forward so that future generations of Christian men will say, "What a dynamic future there is for me in the church!"

PART I

A FORLORN CHALLENGE:
The Unchurched Man

Chapter 1

Where Are the Men?

On April 6, 1812, Lord Wellington's 25,000 allied soldiers stood ready to assault the French-held fortress of Badajoz, Spain. It would become one of the bloodiest advances in the Napoleonic wars.

For a solid month, English heavy artillery had battered the walls, 18 and 24-pound balls of iron smashing into a few choice spots in the stonework and gates. From the wall tops, General Philippon and his 5,000 French troops looked down with anxious faces.

The bombarding gunners sought to blast out a little niche that would widen, ever so gradually, to the point that a few outrageously brave men might dare scramble up the rubble together and charge into the breach. So, relentlessly, day and night, iron hurled through the air until the barrels of Wellington's howitzers glowed red.

Slowly a hole began to open.

All around the fort the French had dug trenches. Some they filled with water. In other spots, winding ditches held merciless *chevaux de frise* in their depths. These were the infamous log "horses" covered with projecting swords, ready to shred any falling soldier.

Within the ranks of the attackers, men sat waiting for a call to ring out. They steeled themselves for it, the words of invitation both frightening and powerfully attractive at the same time: *Who will be the first to go? Who will be the first to charge that hole in the castle wall?*

The big guns ceased as the sun went down, for this would be a night raid. In the shadows of firelight, as the call came to their ears, a few of the men stood, fixed their bayonets and walked forward.

What kind of man would take a walk like that? For in those days the small battalions of the "first to go in" bore a special name: the Forlorn Hope.

Forlorn Hope. . . or Hopeful Future?

In the pages ahead I invite you to consider the future of men and the church. Some would say that "forlorn hope" sums it up—that the leaders of men's ministry fight a losing battle, that they face massive walls and impenetrable gates. They may be filled with courage, but with what hope of success?

That outlook has statistical support. David Murrow, at his website *www.churchformen.com*[1], lays it out:

- **The typical U.S. congregation draws an adult crowd that's 61% female, 39% male. This gender gap shows up in all age categories.**
- **On any given Sunday there are 13 million more adult women than men in America's churches.**
- **This Sunday almost 25% of married, churchgoing women will worship without their husbands.**
- **Over 70% of the boys who are being raised in church will abandon it during their teens and twenties. Many of these boys will never return.**

- **More than 90% of American men believe in God and five out of six call themselves Christians. But only one out of six attend church on a given Sunday.**
- **Fewer than 10% of U.S. churches are able to establish or maintain a vibrant men's ministry.**

Men and the church: a daunting challenge? Absolutely.

However, when I ask what kind of man responds to the challenge of fortress breaking, I think of one like the apostle Peter. I imagine him as he stood before his Master and heard these weighty words: "I will build my church, and the gates of hell shall not prevail against it" (Matthew 16:18, KJV). I envision Jesus holding Peter's gaze for many heartbeats, making the force of that statement sink deeply into a beloved man's heart.

In that poignant scene is the cure for any potential despair about our future together in the church. In light of Jesus's declaration, I take comfort in a simple observation: *gates are not offensive weapons.* Gates are strictly for defense, as at the fortress of Badajoz. That means the church isn't a passive entity in Jesus's view. It's an active, attacking force, thrusting itself against the walls and gates of Hades—or whatever seeks to thwart the kingdom of God.

That fortress looming before us is another kind of "kingdom", of course. It resides on earth for the time being and holds the living soul-dead, the addicted, the friendless, the despairing, the hurting, the seeking, the divorcing, the sinning, the bored and the uninspired, all of whom are looking, consciously or not, for real life.

This kingdom also encloses the average guy who's just doing the best he can, mildly satisfied with his job during the day and with a few hours of TV at night. It holds Christian men, some who see church as another role to play or one more obligation in a busy week. It also holds the man of goodwill and optimistic attitude who might like to be invited into a fellowship of mission, as well as any guy who stands on the outskirts of a congregation, looking in, secretly wanting to belong.

However, for our purposes, be assured: it holds every man who hasn't yet been fully grasped by the call of Jesus: "Drop what you are holding on to, what seems to be saving you at the moment, and follow Me."

In my 25 years of ministry to men in the church, I have developed a passion for reaching into that realm and a heartfelt compassion for any man who inhabits it at any level. I've come to see that the church has a heroic Personage to lead it within those walls. He has already conquered decisively, by means of an unlikely tactic—a conquering by self-surrender. You see, the church advances through pure self-sacrifice. A cross leads us and the attack is an assault of love. This ancient hymn of the church proclaims it with poetic majesty:

> **Let this mind be in you,**
> **which was also in Christ Jesus:**
> **Who, being in the form of God,**
> **thought it not robbery**
> **to be equal with God:**
> **But made himself of no reputation,**
> **and took upon him the form of a servant,**
> **and was made in the likeness of men:**
> **And being found in fashion as a man,**
> **he humbled himself,**
> **and became obedient unto death,**
> **even the death of the cross.**
> **Wherefore God also hath highly exalted him,**
> **and given him a name**
> **which is above every name:**
> **That at the name of Jesus**
> **Every knee should bow,**

> **of things in heaven, and things in earth,
> and things under the earth;
> And that every tongue should confess
> that Jesus Christ is Lord,
> to the glory of God the Father.**

Philippians 2:5-11(KJV)

Here is a vision of a hopeful future—*guaranteed.* It moves us forward by self-giving, with the goal of transforming kingdoms of darkness into the kingdom of light. And that is why I'm so passionate about ministry to men and so hopeful about its effectiveness and that is why I wrote this book. I've found that working for the *transformation of men's hearts* is one of the greatest joys in this life. "I came that they might have life," said Jesus, "and have it in abundance." I want that kind of life. I want to know it in myself and I rejoice in seeing it flourish in other men.

The Future Is Here: Courageous Leadership!

Now let's get perfectly practical. You've picked up this book. Why?

It's true that much has been written about ministry to men in recent years, beginning with the advent of the modern Men's Movement in the late 1980s. A few key books set the stage, such as Pat Morley's *The Man in the Mirror* (1989), Robert Bly's *Iron John: A Book about Men* (1990) and Robert Hicks's *The Masculine Journey* (1993). Then came Promise Keepers and a cascade of books, conferences, programs and tapes. Since then, mountains of material have been generated—to God's glory!—and you can find a good introduction to many of these in Appendix A of this book. I certainly have my recommended favorites in the current day.

So the obvious question stands: With all this material available, why *this* book and who needs to read it? Consider for a moment just four men I know:

- **Scenario:** *I just landed here; now what?* You are a 55-year-old Episcopal priest who's just been called to serve a small parish in southwest Florida. You immediately notice that in this church, as in many you've known over the years, active involvement is mostly a "woman's thing". The altar guild ladies are hard workers, the prayer shawl knitting circle is thriving, and the lay Eucharistic ministers are dedicated and reliable. But where are the men? You've reached the point in your life where you'd like to do something about this situation. *Surely Christian men want to have significant ministry, too.* But what, exactly, are you going to do?

- **Scenario:** *I'm stuck with making the breakfast again?* You're a guy, age 43, who's been meeting at the church with six other men on Friday mornings for the past eight years. Actually, you're considered the leader of this little group. You enjoy the camaraderie, the frequent laughter and the chance to toss around some ideas about life and religion. You supply an interesting newspaper article each week for discussion and you especially enjoy the weekly bacon, eggs and biscuits. In fact, lately you've mused, *Seems like I'm mainly coming for the food—or because it's my turn to cook!* Shouldn't there be more to this men's small-group thing? But how do you proceed?

- **Scenario:** *I could use a few guy friends—little help here!* You've been sitting in the same pew for the last six months of Sundays, which is a real accomplishment in itself. You're a 36-year-old dad, divorced, but going out with a woman who has three young children of her own. You've got relationship problems to high heaven—with parents, kids, ex-spouse and even the new girlfriend. But you went to a men's retreat with a friend from another church and came back totally inspired to start a new way of life, a Christ-dedicated life. Hence the last half year in church. *Shouldn't this place be helping me with my newfound commitment—helping me to know what it really means to be a Christian man, a good husband, a father, and a disciple?*

You look around and see a couple of other guys who might be thinking some of the same things. You're willing to get something started with them along the lines of a "men's group". But what steps should you take?

- **Scenario:** *She's dragging me to church again! I waited all week for this NFL extravaganza. And since we live on the West Coast, the whole thing starts just about the time my wife's pastor begins preaching. Okay, I can handle it most Sundays, but today, of all days, she gets it in her head that I "just have to be there." I'm 26, just married, and there's going to be a big fight; I can feel it coming on. What I haven't told my wife is that—surprisingly to me—I have noticed a pretty cool group of men in attendance at this church who have engaged me in conversation and actually invited me to some of their events. I don't want to become "churchy", but truthfully feel I could use some help—maybe make some new friends. What is my right next step?*

In my work I've done a lot of traveling to churches and visiting with just these types of men. One thing I keep hearing goes something like this: "Jay, I know there's a ton of material out there about men, but it's overwhelming. Where do I start, so that I can know the next steps for me, *right here in my denominational church?*"

Here is where I want to put into your hands an inspiring and practical book that simply says, "Welcome. I'd like to introduce you to the future of the church and how it abounds with men doing meaningful ministry for their Lord." I want to give you a book that shows you the crisis-level **problem** of absentee men (Part 1), offers the **solution** (Part 2), *which is to become expert at welcoming them back;* and shows what a man would **look like** (Part 3), if he were indeed to come back and be discipled by your church, in your particular denomination, into a deeper spiritual life.

So, if you are one of those four men above—a pastor, a current men's leader, an aspiring "gatherer of men" or a reluctant participant—then this book is the place to get started in your quest to welcome men back to the church. It's true that no single book can cover the vast topic of "all things men", but I'll show you a bit of what's out there and give you an idea of how to enter this ministry arena.

The Mundane Battle: A Willing Heart

Now let's go back to the siege of Badajoz and the self-sacrificing company of men called the Forlorn Hope. On that moonlit night of April 6, those men moved forward into the teeth of withering gunfire. Many of them quickly fell to French mines, mortars and muskets. As the flag bearers were wounded or killed, their fellow soldiers reached down to give encouraging words, nurse the wounded and take up the flag-staffs themselves. Up ahead the leaders slogged up the jagged stones, through the smoke, heads down, teeth set, up, up, up.

This was a band of men willing to risk all for the greater reward. It was army policy that those few who survived the assault would indeed receive spectacular compensation. Privates immediately were elevated to the rank of officers and officers would move to the next level, no questions asked. The most amazing thing about the Forlorn Hope battalions was that *some men literally demanded to join.*

It's amazing what can happen when men see a chance to respond to the heroic mission, even against impossible odds. Yet those men at Badajoz looked for earthly rewards. The Christian leader who gives himself to the challenge of ministry to men looks not at the landscape with a hope of personal gain, but with an eye toward a still invisible heavenly hope—what the Bible calls the "blessed hope". This is the return of our Savior, who will come to set the world right and hand out a few crowns.

My dear brothers and sisters in Christ, whatever else motivates and energizes you, surely at the heart of it is the potential for *this* great reward—to hear, on the day when you stand before Him, "Well done, good and faithful servant" (Matthew 25:21). If any of us Christian leaders sit and dwell long enough with the question, *"Why am I doing all of this?"* we will feel the compelling attraction of that day.

Leader, are you ready to take up the banner and advance? It will require a deepening compassion for men and their needs. Your weapons are those of Christ Himself as He walked upon the earth: truth, love, kindness, friendship, the extension of mercy and grace and an unfettered joy:

> *"Be of good cheer; I have overcome the world"*
> *(John 16:33).*

In other words, you advance with an infectious enthusiasm for the truths of God and an unrelenting encouragement to join the works of God.

This is where all battle imagery fails us and quickly falls away. For the goal is not destruction and not even victory, which is already won, but the Christian formation of men. Compared to ancient siege warfare, that might seem rather unexciting if it weren't for the fact that it is the very way the church will enter its future. It begins *with a leader's willing heart* to take a sincere interest in the ordinary lives of the ordinary men around him.

- **Are you willing to build a relationship with *that* quiet man?**
- **Could you help *this* young guy get involved in improving his marriage?**
- **Might you plan a study with *those* men on how to become better fathers?**
- **Suppose you asked *him* to go fishing with you, or jog in the morning, or see a ballgame? Could you begin pouring your life and wisdom into him?**
- **And how about taking one guy to lunch and asking, "How are you doing? No, *really*, how are you doing?" Would you have the courage to just listen for a while?**

You get the idea and you could add your own scenarios right where you live. Again, this is the real battle: the leader courageously deciding to take action, by the power of God's Spirit, for the spiritual growth of men in the church. At Church of the Redeemer in Sarasota, Florida, we sum up the mission like this:

> **Encouraging men,**
> **through relationships,**
> **to seek Christ-centered living.**

Now, how does all this look in the most practical terms? Here's a hint. It looks a lot like your church and the guy next to you in the pew, or the guy who *could* be there; it looks like you and him together. In our next chapter let's consider who he is in our culture today.

Your Next-Step Action Plan

IDEA. Why not begin your study of this book with a renewed commitment to personal prayer? And if your heart is moved with compassion for the men around you who need to grow in Christ, consider fasting for a period of time. In daily times of silence, hold this intention before Almighty God: *"Prepare my heart for ministry, O Lord!"*

For Personal Reflection

1. When have I felt the call to a mission that seemed impossible? How did I respond? And what is that mission at the moment?

2. As a leader of men, or an emerging leader, in what specific areas do I need more courage? What things tend to keep me "stuck" or glued to the ground when I sense Christ's call to "move out"?

3. What most inspires me with energy for working with men? Who can I call on to partner with me—two by two—to pursue this big holy, audacious adventure?

4. What particular gifts, talents and opportunities has God placed in my life for effectively working with men? What first step could I take with one of those opportunities?

For Group Discussion

1. In building a case for hope, when it comes to the future of men in the church, have the ideas in this chapter succeeded? Why or why not? What ideas would you add, either to give more hope or more caution? Talk about it!

2. Flash forward in history 20 years and imagine your church on Sunday morning. How many men are there? *Why* are they there—or not there?

3. In your understanding, what is the "decisive victory" of Jesus? Tell a little bit about what this victory means to you—in theological terms and in everyday living.

4. To what extent do you agree or disagree with the idea that even Christian men can inhabit a kingdom that actually *hinders* the expansion of God's kingdom? Check out these Scripture passages: John 15:10; 1 Corinthians 3:1-4; Ephesians 4:14; Romans 6:1; Romans 8:6.

5. Look again at the bulleted list of "sincere" ways we might reach out to another man for fellowship and/or mentoring. On a scale of 1 to 5, where are you on the "Willing Heart Meter"?

1_____ 2 _____ 3_____4 _____ 5

No way I'm   I'm Ready,
getting involved!   willing, able!

Chapter 2

Who Are These Guys Today?

You know the guy. He somehow managed to graduate college, but he still lives with his parents. And he doesn't plan to move out anytime soon. Or maybe he has a decent job. He lives with some buddies in the city. But he blows most of his money on video games and his latest efforts to bring a girl back to his place.
—**Collin Hansen**[1]

Beginning in about 1965, men have been slipping out the side doors of our mainline denominational churches, taking their families with them. And they are not returning.

So let's ask ourselves, *"Who are these guys?"* What are their needs and desires and what are the culture's challenges and opportunities for them? Perhaps we can learn how best to welcome them back.

One thing we know: the man of today is *not* the man of yesteryear. One pastor put it like this:

> Before we start singing "We are one in the Spirit, we are one in the Lord," here's the harsher reality—we are brothers on the same ship called "The Titanic"... We are competing largely for the hearts and minds of the 20 and 30-somethings with their iPads and

macchiatos. We are already dinosaurs and we did not know it. The average Christian in the world right now is an African or Latin American female in her early 20s. . . The world has moved on, God has moved on and we didn't even notice.[2]

As spiritual leaders, we're looking to develop relationships with men and to foster relationships *among* men, for spiritual transformation. Simply put, we want to know and help the men around us as they labor to find their place in our rapidly changing world. So if the denominational church is to have a future, it might be good to keep an eye on the up-and-coming generations. If you were born before 1970, their world is quite different from yours.

Traditional Manhood and the New Normal

Remember how it was? We once had much more clarity about manhood. Not too long ago there were certain "givens" about the male identity. Going back to the "greatest generation" and up through the 1960s, popular television shows and movies expressed it pretty clearly.

The GOOD MAN was like Mr. Smith: he led the Boy Rangers until he "went to Washington." He was a man of integrity, a man of his word.

The GOOD HUSBAND was like Ward Cleaver: he worked as a dependable provider, thoroughly predictable and upright, a source of wisdom and strength.

The GOOD FATHER was like Jim Anderson in *Father Knows Best*: he always seemed ready with solid wisdom, able to give sage advice to the kids in their crises.

The GOOD CITIZEN was like Andy of Mayberry: he had a mature outlook, was respected in the community, a role model to his son.

The GOOD HERO was like Roy Rogers: he might have to fight you, but if he knocked you down, he'd let you get up before resuming the brawl.

Leaving aside the question of whether such depictions were realistic, we do know this is how Hollywood *wanted* to portray men. Whether or not such ideals were actually reached in real life, we knew there *was* an ideal and society seemed to aspire to it. There was an expected worthiness to a man. He dressed in a way that showed he valued his personal dignity, for instance. What man of that day would go out to dinner or board an airplane without donning a nice suit and tie? The man carried himself as if he were indeed mature, responsible and someone of weighty substance, no matter his occupation.

Here's my point: Not many decades ago, manhood was widely understood as the result of going through certain stages to maturity, accomplishing certain developmental tasks and navigating certain expected transitions by gaining particular skills. Our society seemed just naturally to know this. According to Robert Wuthnow, a prominent research sociologist, there are five key "developmental tasks" that were once achieved much more smoothly by young men:

1. **leaving home**
2. **finishing school**
3. **becoming financially independent**
4. **getting married**
5. **having a child**

Accomplish those five tasks and you had entered society's idea of manhood. But at least since the **Boomer** generation (born 1946–1964), the succeeding generations of **Busters** (1965–83) and **Mosaics** (1984–2002) have taken a much more winding pathway—or gotten lost along the way!—to mature manhood. In fact, many young men today simply postpone their entry into

34

adulthood. It's now called the *odyssey years*—this unnaturally extended time period between youth and adulthood.

Consider it statistically.[3] In 1960, 77% of women and 65% percent of men had completed all these tasks—had become adults—by age thirty. But in our day, only 46% of women and 31% of men have completed all the tasks by the time they reach 30 years of age. In other words, today the *majority* of younger men are floating somewhere in Odyssey World!

The question is whether the denominational church of today is ready to disciple today's younger man—and equip its older men to become disciplers in this new world. "Most of the young adults who don't fit the normal Christian married mold are lovingly called 'pagans' by others and sent my way," says one teacher in a Chicago congregation. "But I love 'em and work hard to disciple them in new ways. I think they are the 'new normal' Christians."[4]

David Brooks, in a *New York Times* column, speaks of this new-normal odyssey as "a decade of wandering" between adolescence and adulthood. Because of it, we have delayed marriage, delayed childbirth and delayed careers (or never-launched vocations). "Dating gives way to Facebook and hooking up," says Brooks. "Marriage gives way to cohabitation. Church attendance gives way to spiritual longing. Newspaper reading gives way to blogging. . . [and] there is every reason to think this phase will grow more pronounced in the coming years."[5]

In 1970, 69% of 25 year old and 85% of 30 year old white men were married. By 2000 those numbers were down to 33% and 58%. Between 2000 and 2006 alone, the median age of marriage for men climbed nearly one year, from 26.8 to 27.5.[6] Collin Hansen, writer for *Christianity Today*, asks: "Can our churches afford to wait at least 12 years, between ages 18 and 30, for men to return?"

Are all men on this odyssey path? Of course not! But, in fact, the age of the average churchman in an American congregation is a lot older than thirty. If we have grasped this "new normal" world, we'll have a good handle on a large part of the unchurched, missing-man problem. *He's mostly a young guy somewhere between adolescence and adulthood and he may be much older than you think.*

When it comes to reaching him, we've got to remember that our culture has moved away from surety about the journey to manhood and this has caused much confusion in the hearts of men today. They aren't so sure of their "tasks" anymore, they are getting stuck in moving through life and they are wondering about their true identity.

According to the 2010 USA Census statistics, the majority of Americans are under 40 years old (and the largest group is young 20-somethings). In other words, there is often a huge age difference between a community's civil and religious leaders and the average citizen. As one teen lamented, "Grandpa is making all my clothing decisions!" Yet, such statistics include a big note of encouragement for church leaders: the largest and most receptive unchurched demographic are those same 20-somethings. And according to Barna Research, receptivity to the gospel tends to decrease with age.

Reaching Generation "Nice"

For myriad young men today, religion is "a very nice thing", demanding no real commitment. Christian Smith and Melinda Denton, in *Soul Searching,* termed it Moralistic Therapeutic Deism (MTD), a "hodgepodge of banal, self-serving, feel-good beliefs yield[ing] a default spirituality that bears little resemblance to the historic teachings of Christianity."[7]

Listen to one young man, in the comments section under a USA Today article titled "Survey: 72% of Millennials 'more spiritual than religious.'" He describes himself as male, age 28, a mechanical engineer and "rather patient, except with the truly ignorant and disrespectful," a libertarian and agnostic.

> As a member of this age group that has fallen away from religion, I can honestly say that most of it was due to those who would "preach" their own interpreted message, but could not comprehend what they were actually saying/portraying. As if one flawed human's interpretation is so much better than any other flawed human's interpretation. . . There really are no fundamental differences between faith A and faith B. . . Live and let live. . . Why should what I think make ANY difference in what you think? Your beliefs shouldn't require me to think the same and vice versa. If they do, then something is very, very wrong.[8]

If we're to reach this kind of man, we'll need to pay attention to researchers like Kenda Dean, who argues that a renewal of faith within American young people depends upon churches' ability to *recover a sense of mission*. In *Almost Christian*, Dean found that the most committed young people in the National Study of Youth and Religion shared four important traits: they could tell a personal and powerful story about God, they belonged to a significant faith community, they exhibited a sense of vocation and they possessed a profound sense of hope. Based on these findings, Dean proposes an approach to Christian education that *places mission at its core*.[9]

The bottom line is this: Jesus did not call people to come to church, although commitment to Jesus ultimately leads us to commitment to the church. He called people to follow Him. I'm all about challenging the church to hear that personal call from Jesus and to take it to men, both in structured programming and in one-to-one discipleship.

A more faithful church is the solution to the "new normal" and Moralistic Therapeutic Deism. God, above all, is much more than "nice". He is the Almighty who asks for our very lives. As C. S. Lewis once said, "Christianity, if false, is of no importance, and if true, of infinite importance. The only thing it cannot be is moderately important."[10]

On a hopeful note, I hear a man like Thom Rainer, president and CEO of LifeWay Christian Resources, telling us something crucial in a recent blog post. Based on his company's extensive research, he points to a trend of deeper commitment among many millennials.

> **Although the relative number of Christians in this generation is small, those who are Christians are *more likely to have a radical commitment to the gospel* than Christians in previous American generations. Millennial Christians will not settle for business as usual in our churches. They will not be content with going through the motions, programs without a purpose, and spectator Christianity. They take their faith seriously, and they have little patience with churches that focus most of their resources on the members. These Millennials are serious about taking the gospel to the nations and to their communities.[111]**

Be encouraged and challenged here! It is often said the youth are the future of our church. Stated more accurately, if faith isn't taught and caught by our youth from equipped Christian adults, the future of the church looks mighty small. So, if you are an older guy, you may be thinking that it's super difficult to develop a mentoring relationship with a young man in your church. But have you tried it? You will be surprised—perhaps even blown away—by how hungry these guys are for just this kind of relationship.

Test me here; try it. All my experience tells me that when an older, more mature Christian determines to overcome his reluctance to approach that young man (who may have spiked hair, or tattoos, or wear his pants a little low), the response is positive. Yes, many younger guys are more than willing to be mentored. They know they need help to grow into manhood. They're looking for some wise direction along the pathway to Christian maturity. So, don't be the gray-hair that shrugs and says, "Hey, I just can't relate to this new generation." That's a cop-out. You are called to try. And if you are sincere and willing to be transparent, you'll succeed.

STORY FROM THE MISSION FIELD

JAY CROUSE

Jeff Kern and I have been longtime buddies in the mission field of ministry to men in our families, church and community. Little did we know that our years of experience would be equipping us for a very important opportunity to mentor a special young man.

In the fall of 2011, Jeff's daughter, Maggie, began dating Caleb Stevens. Caleb and Jeff immediately hit it off for a couple of reasons. At the top of the list was their shared passion, as former Ohioans, for the Ohio State Buckeyes.

In getting to know this 27-year-old, Jeff began to sense that Caleb could benefit from a mentoring relationship. However, since Caleb was dating his daughter, Jeff realized he was not the right person for the job. He needed to reach out to someone else to pursue this potential mentoring relationship. In time, Jeff asked Caleb if he would like to meet his longtime, spiritual brother—me! Caleb was curious and interested.

In January of 2012, Jeff and Caleb met me at my office to get acquainted and "check each other out." The meeting went very well. I was drawn to Caleb because he was faithful, available, teachable and stable (FATS). From that initial meeting, Caleb and I set a time to continue our conversation. Let me point out, too, that I firmly believe that men should mentor or disciple only other men. A man mentoring a woman, other than a family member, is unintentionally courting disaster.

Over the next months, Caleb and I met regularly to sort through vital issues in his life, his career, his past, further education options, his faith and his wonderful, emerging relationship with Maggie.

I have discovered in mentoring relationships that at some point it is most helpful to strongly encourage your protégé to set aside time to develop their own plan of action. To that end, I have relied on a time-tested, six-hour, personal, spiritual retreat format. From experience, I know this time set aside for prayer, discernment and reflection will give my protégé the opportunity to review all the ground we have covered and develop his own plan for the next year.

I suggested this planning retreat idea to Caleb and within a couple of months he was ready to pursue this "road less traveled". He took this retreat planning process seriously and enjoyed a very successful goal-setting time.

What a joy it was to receive a call from Caleb in November of 2012. He and Maggie were preparing their wedding plans for December 23, 2012 and they would be honored if I would speak at their wedding.

Mentoring is a life-giving experience that allows you the amazing and fulfilling opportunity to invest in the life of a younger man.

My point in this chapter has been to wake us up to the unchurched man and who he is. I've focused on younger men because they are obviously our hope for the future church. They will be our "missed opportunity" if denominational churches aren't equipped to reach and mentor them.

We've made a start in this exploration, but we need to go deeper. What we've looked at so far is simply evidence that the overall cultural context of postmodernism has pervaded the being of many of the men who no longer attend our churches. In the chapter ahead, we'll look at some obstacles this philosophy puts in the way of welcoming men back into the church.

Your Next-Step Action Plan

PLAN TO DO SOME INTERVIEWS. Consider sitting down with some men you know. Choose several men who are in different stages in the life cycle. Ask them to tell you about their view of manhood and how they came to their understanding. How do they view their current roles in society and in the church? Your real-life investigations will help you in your ministry to men!

For Personal Reflection

1. For me, personally, is "manhood" a fuzzy concept or clearly defined? Think about it.

2. What moves me to have compassion for men today?

3. What men in my world could benefit from my prayers? How will I pray for them right now?

4. What next step could I take in reaching out to one of these men in personal friendship?

5. What is my main takeaway from this chapter—the best way for me to apply it in practical action?

For Group Discussion

1. In contrasting the tasks of "traditional manhood" with the "odyssey years" pathway of many young men today, to what extent do you agree with the analysis given in this chapter? What would you add to the mix?

2. How have you observed the traditional roles and tasks of manhood being played out in the lives of men in your world lately?

3. Share about some specific instances when you have observed in a man a lifestyle that contrasts with traditional manhood. What are your conclusions about the pros and cons in this way of being a man?

4. What practical responses to the culture seem right for you and the men in your church? Talk about it in the most practical terms possible. Can you develop some plans together?

Chapter 3

What's Their Cultural Challenge?

These [postmodern] men aren't so different from everyone else. They need the gospel to liberate them from themselves, so that they will seek first the kingdom, not the latest Will Ferrell movie. If we expect to see these men in our churches, perhaps we should begin by looking at ourselves to see whether we model the discipleship we profess. We do these men no favors if we transfer them from the kingdom of video games into the kingdom of conspicuous consumerism.

—**Collin Hansen** [1]

A re real men the Gordon Gekko-type business moguls, loudly proclaiming, "Greed is good"? Or are we nurses? Are we the Marlboro man, or do real men knit? Are we sports and hunting wild men, or are we pursuing our wives' desires for us to "be more sensitive"? Or should we try to embody and live out all of these expectations?

Today, "the real man" is being defined and redefined by individuals in a philosophical culture fundamentally different from that of our grandparents and their forebears. How can we describe this culture?

Postmodernism Encounters the Male Identity

No generalization of the postmodern philosophy can do it justice in one book chapter. However, to be better prepared in your work with unchurched men, some of whom are saturated in this cultural worldview, be sure you know its basics.

- **It's built largely on *subjectivity and relativism*.** The idea of objective truth, or moral absolutes of any kind, has been largely abandoned by popular culture. If we buy into this way of living, we are left to make our own "truth for me." What feels right for each individual is right. If we sincerely seek and "find our own path," we have done something laudable. But what does that do for the question, "What is a man?"

In effect, post modernity leaves everything up for grabs; no generalizations are really possible. All is individual and thus, each man must redefine what it means to be human and to be male. Sadly, the shapers of our common culture today (i.e., the television execs!) often move us to the lowest common denominator. Consider just one TV sitcom that's all about men, who also mentor a younger man: *Two and a Half Men*. What does this show tell us about how we are asked to view men? First, a word from the Parent's Television Council:

> *Two and a Half Men* **is not appropriate for children of all ages. Language includes "hell", "damn", "bastard", "crap", "ass" and "bitch". Far worse than the frequent use of foul language is the constant barrage of sexual scenes and jokes. Even though Charlie's promiscuous character is gone,**

> **the sexual content has not abated, with jokes about men wearing women's underwear, sexually transmitted diseases, prostitution, threesomes, the size of Walden's genitals and visual and audio sex depictions are rampant. Walden is shown nude with his private areas pixilated. . . .*Two and a Half Men* is not recommended for viewers under age 18.[2]**

As one friend tells me, hearing radio advertisements about upcoming episodes of this show—while riding in the car with one's mother—can be quite embarrassing! But I have great sadness about this and the myriad similar depictions of manhood today. The view of men is grievous to me. The main adult characters are hardly worthy of emulating, yet for Jake, the teen who takes all of this in, the message is clear: becoming a man means having as much sex as possible, with as many women as possible, while pursuing a low-level hedonism toward all potential pleasures, wrapped in a cynical outlook on all traditional values.

The church, of course, is absent in these screenplays. But if religion is ever brought in, it will focus on the spiritual— "spiritual, but not religious"—and in postmodernism, spiritualities are interchangeable. The question of how to get to the top of the mountain for personal salvation is easily answered: choose your own path, for they all lead to the same place.

- **It approaches the world in *nonlinear* and *non-rational* ways.** Have you tried "reasoning" with a postmodern mind? It was once standard procedure to state the *position* we held and then marshal *arguments* in support; now it's how we "feel" about a matter. Then we would show how our arguments logically follow to an inevitable conclusion; now it's me, talking to myself. My debating opponent has moved on to another multitask, with this parting shot as the clincher to verbal victory: "Whatever!"

In light of this new consciousness, teachers, public speakers and even preachers are beginning to reconsider how they arrange their discourses in an attempt to fit with how people search the Web. Why create an introduction, a transition, numbered points and a conclusion? The postmodern speaker knows that a generation raised on the Internet is used to gather information by launching search forays out from a central theme point (imagine a circle with arrows pointing out from it). One moves from the various "theme points" outward into related topics, then back again, then to another theme point with various arrows pointing out into other themes, which lead to still other "links". This book is built on the older, linear model—are you still with me here?

Again, go to most any college classroom and you will encounter multitasking on a monumental scale: students texting while surfing the Web, while answering emails, while listening to the lecturer, who easily switches between PowerPoint, handouts, Q & A and neighbor-nudge. When students write their papers, they will tap out a paragraph here and there, the task sandwiched between other tasks. The upshot is if you are over forty, you are a stranger in a foreign land; your mind is wired for a different way of experiencing reality.

Now please hear this clearly: the non-rational part of you is an important part! Information comes to us not just in logically ordered propositions. Indeed, Jesus Himself never wrote a book, nor did He confine Himself to a lecture series. He touched people, their hearts and bodies. He sought to move them through their imaginations and emotions. But He did declare Himself to be *the* Truth and *the* Light.

- **It is an existence lived strictly *in the now*.** For those immersed in the postmodern approach to life, the past is hardly as important as it once was. What worth is there to "ancient history" or even a minimal understanding of the 20ᵗʰ century, if it doesn't impact me right here and now? The past is there primarily for deconstructing, because of a key assumption: the enlightenment of human beings proceeds on an evolutionary path of progress.

This means, according to postmodernism, that in each new century, people are smarter, wiser and more intelligent than the preceding generations. What could an ancient tell us about life, sans scientific investigation, that we don't already know in a "deeper way", with subtle, seeing-both-sides nuances that would have baffled the wise men of the past? All the up-to-date info is at our fingertips *right now*. What could a Renaissance theologian tell us about existence that the Hubble spacecraft hasn't uncovered to an infinitely greater degree?

Like a chameleon whose colors change to match the background against which it moves, the individual fluidly glides across the landscape of time, continually altered in body and spirit by the energy of the present.[3]

Is everything about postmodernism bad? No. For example, it is good to let go of any old ways of being that have proven ineffective, insufficient, superficial, destructive, or just plain wrong about reality. Sacred cows are best left for dead. In addition, many, many people who hold no sense of objective truth are, nevertheless, on a sincere quest to find what "makes sense" in the world. They want to know how to live in a way that brings them and others peace, justice and harmony. Many are more than willing to be open, vulnerable and transparent, which makes them utterly attractive. Such unchurched men are a delight to relate to, because they are on a laudable pursuit.

A sincere and honest look at life is always good in human beings. Here is where we can meet men in a warm and engaging way, creating friendships for the simple reason that we *want* them as friends. In the process, the Christ who lives in us will no doubt rub off on them a bit—and we, in turn, will learn some things!

OUR POST-CHRISTIAN WORLD

Culture is evolving and Christianity no longer occupies the center of public discourse. Post-Christendom is the culture that emerges as the Christian faith loses coherence within a society that has been shaped by its story. *Here are some of the transitions as post-Christendom takes root.*[4]

From the center to the margins: The Christian story and the churches, once central in societal consciousness, move to the outskirts with many other worldviews.
From the majority to the minority: Christians move from the (often overwhelming) majority into minority status.
From settlers to sojourners: Christians, who once felt at home in a culture shaped by their story, are aliens, exiles and pilgrims in a culture where they no longer feel at home.
From privilege to plurality: Christians who once enjoyed many privileges are now merely one community among many.
From control to witness: Churches could once exert much control over society, but now we exercise influence only through witnessing to our story and its implications.
From maintenance to mission: In Christendom, the emphasis was on maintaining a supposedly Christian status quo, but in post-Christendom it is on mission within a contested environment.

From institution to movement: Churches once operated mainly in *institutional* mode, but in post-Christendom the church again must become a Christian *movement*.

Clearly, our postmodern, post-Christendom culture significantly subverts the traditional expectations, stages and transitions that males must still trek if they are to choose to mature. How? By giving us ever decreasing numbers of examples, or "models", that show how healthy maturing to manhood would look in our day and by constantly questioning the idea that any *one* model—the biblical ideal for example—could actually apply to many specific individuals in aggregate and possibly to a whole culture.

Nevertheless, the church must help men mature and grow and travel through the responsible stages in spite of our relativistic culture today. It must provide models in the lives of real-life mentors. After all, we are Christians, people of the objective, historical, incarnate Word. The great thing is that the church can meet men at the crossroads and help them in their confusion.

So, specifically, what has this virtual dismantling of the tradition done to men? I admit to you, at the risk of sounding ever so curmudgeon-like, that I believe post modernity is hostile to traditional masculinity. It is therefore contributing to dysfunction and dismay among men, especially the younger generations. Consider just four symptoms.

As we've seen, many younger men exhibit an **inability to mature.** This is understandable, for who is helping them see what mature manhood is? With little objective understanding of the characteristics, roles and responsibilities of adult manhood, many young men extend their adolescence. Have you seen any of these guys—the 35-year-olds with droopy pants on skateboards—at the mall parking lot lately? This is an aspect of what has commonly been called role confusion. According to Barbara Engler in her book *Personality Theories*, it's "the inability to conceive of oneself as a productive member of one's own society." It's a danger for society, because it often occurs in adolescence, especially when it's time to get a job.[5]

Today's men are **hard-pressed to point to laudable heroes and mentors** to follow as they make their way through life. Who are our heroes for men today? Mostly we have celebrities before us in the media and the main media approach to celebrity status is to find a way to tear it down. How will the ever-growing parade of morally tainted fallen "heroes" lead our young men through the stages and tasks of adulthood? The best of our baseball heroes get caught with drugs and prominent politicians are discovered doing strange things in bathroom stalls. Where is the sense of personal worth and dignity? May we love the young men who seek heroes today. May we have compassion on them—and find ways to be a personal hero to many of them.

Younger men often seem **unable to construct a powerful moral center**. Outside of the church, where does one go for moral certitude? The "spirituality" movements won't give us this, yet without it, a man becomes either fearful or unrestrained. He will implode with anxiety or explode without boundaries, hurting lives in the process.

Men may well **wonder how to take their part in effective civil leadership.** It used to be understood that women were in charge of the "private world" at home. Men were normally the leaders in public, pursuing civil excellence in their work and in community leadership. This has changed. Women are now ever present in the workplace and in civic leadership. I recall watching a 1950s movie in which the boss was speaking on the phone in front of his secretary: "Have your girl call my girl."

This was normal conversation, right or wrong, but it did give a stable framework for role definition. Robert Lewis, in his *Quest for Authentic Manhood* video series, says that our increasingly feminized culture has actually *emasculated* the warrior in many young men. "The result has been the creation of the soft male, indecisive as to direction, weak as to leadership."[6]

The Way Out: Authentic Christian Manhood

Lewis doesn't stop with critique; he defines authentic Christian manhood in terms of four "manhood principles"[7]

> **Manhood Principle #1:** A real man rejects passivity.
> **Manhood Principle #2:** A real man accepts responsibility.
> **Manhood Principle #3:** A real man leads courageously.
> **Manhood Principle #4:** A real man expects the greater reward.

The authentic man is active in pursuing and promoting kingdom values in his world, starting within himself and his own family. He takes responsibility for his actions, confessing his sins, being accountable to others, refusing to shift blame, no matter how difficult his circumstances. He is willing to cast the vision for others, pointing the way forward in his family and community, trusting God as his ultimate guide. This man is accustomed to delaying gratification for the better and greater joy—the "crown" he'll receive when he stands before his Lord and Master on the last day (see 1 Corinthians 9:24-27).

Pause to savor this definition of Christian manhood for a moment. Does it ring true to you, in your own observations and experience? Could you think of any better definition?

If today's men are writing their own code of manhood, one individual at a time, we can help them see that it is a defective code, especially as it tends to keep them distant from their Christian band of brothers. Yet a word of caution is in order: let us beware of a combative, "muscular

Christianity" that stands strictly against culture without seeing its great opportunities. We can reach and mentor men in the Christian faith today, just as the apostles and early Christians did in their own Roman culture.

In other words, we can approach all of this positively. It's not "us" versus "them". Imagine how refreshing it is for a man to hear: "Won't you join us? We're a group of guys who believe something because it's *true* (and we can tell you *why* it's true) and we live in a certain way because we've been grasped by the living Truth Himself!"

You see, we can't just go about changing our creeds, our core beliefs, our time-honored traditions to meet these men "where they are". We must find winsome and attractive ways to invite them to be with us "where Jesus is". He never changes and He is the answer for every man. He is Christ, the crucified, whose saving blood is available in all eras. Even the postmodern, post-Christendom man faces the same invitation that has sounded forth across the centuries:

> Then Jesus said to His disciples, "If anyone desires to come after Me, let him deny himself, and take up his cross, and follow Me. For whoever desires to save his life will lose it, but whoever loses his life for My sake will find it."
>
> (Matthew 16:24, 25)

Here is the real hope for reaching the missing men in our mainline churches. It's the hope of the future: Jesus Himself.

Will the men "out there" respond to Him? Before we try to answer, we'll need to delve a little more deeply into their minds and hearts. We need a depth of insight and understanding as we seek to bring them to our Savior.

You see, I believe some of the most important and enduring qualities of "today's man" lie hidden to us in their mental attitudes. Namely, men carry with them some mostly

unexamined assumptions in their thinking. Leader, know these things about men. That's our next chapter.

STORY FROM THE MISSION FIELD

MIKE FORBES

I am writing this story on a Sunday afternoon. Church services attended, my 17-year-old daughter struggling with "teen" issues, 12-year-old son communicating with cryptic shoulder shrugs, a wood floor buckling due to a slow leak that defies discovery and my wife of 20 years being attacked by the toxic "what will they think of us" syndrome. But life is beautiful because today Jesus is my Lord and I know that this is what "really matters". However, it wasn't always this way.

GDO IS LOVE

When I was a young boy, faith, religion and church was something you did for a week during the summer. Mrs. Murrow, the old lady across the street in a small Idaho town would pack my brother and me off to a vacation Bible school, where we made crafts, sang "Jesus Loves Me," and, most important, ate a snack. One project, in particular, I remember. We were instructed to make a frame of Popsicle sticks, paste a picture of Jesus on a light blue paper background and then glue little alphabet pasta letters "God is Love" next to Him. By the time I was done with my craft, I proudly displayed my handiwork to my brother and the teachers who immediately began to laugh and snicker. I had misspelled God. My picture read GDO IS LOVE! Oh, the shame.

As I grew, my relationship with GDO developed. I created my own temple and worship rituals for him. Foremost was a drive to succeed professionally, to make a lot of money, then to find a great, sexy woman to marry, settle down, create two kids, and do it "all by myself". A Self-Made Man!

But the sacrifices and pressures that GDO expected in return were too high. The solitary lifestyle created an insatiable appetite for pornography. Introduced to me at the ripe old age of ten, my unhealthy desire increased and was fanned to a full blaze with the advent of the Internet. Abusing alcohol and sexual promiscuity were common from age 14 on. Needless to say, these habits did not decline as the years passed, following GDO.

By 28, I was, in fact, married to the perfect wife, yet the hold of infidelity grasped my soul, led by a false belief that it was normal for a successful man like me. Seven years later, with two children, I was confronted with the reality of literally being crushed by the weight of the temple I had created to this GDO. . . and I did it, all by myself.

My life was a classic example of a man's walk through the past 20-30 years. Our culture puts so much weight on success at school, sports and career. We value hard work with no need for God. In fact, God is for the weak. But sooner or later in a man's life, working harder doesn't work anymore.

As a young man, I worked hard to please my father and as a married man, I worked even harder to please my wife; but it seemed that the harder I tried, the worse things became. So, as many have done, I gave up trying and turned to those habits that comforted me, yet I was never fully satisfied.

My life was falling apart. GDO was not helping anymore. My wife and I had separated. My children were in dire straits. My business was failing. It was only our attorneys who were very cooperative. My lifelong ambitions were about to become a "loss" in the win-loss column. I just couldn't understand how I had gotten myself into this situation. My solution was a $150/hour therapist. I was hopeful she could solve my problems. For the first time in my life, I started to examine my actions rather than run like a mindless machine. Even though my pride would not allow me to blame myself, I could see the benefits of my soon-to-be ex-wife's need to find some form of spirituality. She needed it. Not me.

Until one day, I met a little angel of a person, a four-foot, eleven-inch fireball of a Christian lady who asked me why I was so unhappy. You see, the Holy Spirit had directed her to ask me this question. It was the first time I had heard GOD "spelled correctly". Fortunately, my angel knew several strong Christian men from her church who were willing to visit with me and talk about GOD in a "manly" way. One at a time, they would pass by and encourage me to read a certain book or a certain scripture. I still had not accepted Christ, but GOD was now working in my life.

(to be continued in chapter 13)

Your Next-Step Action Plan

TELL THEM THANKS. Think about men who have been major positive influences on you and helped you to grow into mature manhood. To the extent that these men are still living and reachable, contact them with a personal note of thanks, either by mail or in person. Let them know that they have made a difference in your life! For any who are no longer living, offer a prayer of thanks for their lives.

For Personal Reflection

1. How has my "identity as a man" been shaped over the years?

2. Who and what were the early influences on me—as to how to grow into manhood? What were their effects, for good or ill?

3. To what degree has postmodern philosophy found its way into my own worldview?

4. Where does my outlook on manhood clash or conform to what I know of Christian teaching?

For Group Discussion

1. Where do you notice the greatest effects of postmodern philosophy in your world these days?

2. In your opinion, what does it take to help a younger man take up a serious critique of postmodern culture?

3. Name some TV shows or movies that your group is familiar with and discuss how they portray a positive or negative view of men/manhood.

4. Who are your heroes? Why? Name some contemporary men who could be heroes to the younger men in your church.

5. What is your response to the four manhood principles given in this chapter? Tell how you have lived these in your life so far or how you'd like to improve.

Chapter 4

What's in Their Minds?

THE AVERAGE MALE . . .

Is 5' 9" tall and 173 pounds.
Is married, 1.8 years older than his wife and would marry her again.
Has not completed college.
Prefers showering to taking a bath.
Spends about 7.2 hours a week eating.
Does not know his cholesterol count, but it's 211.
Watches 26 hours and 44 minutes of TV a week.
Takes out the garbage in his household.
Prefers white underwear to colored.
Cries about once a month—one fourth as much as Jane Doe.
Falls in love an average of six times during his life.
Eats his corn on the cob in circles, not straight across.
Can't whistle by inserting his fingers in his mouth.
Prefers that his toilet tissue unwind over, rather than under, the spool.
Has sex 2.55 times a week.
Daydreams mostly about sex.
Thinks he looks okay in the nude.
Will not stop to ask for directions when he's in the car.
                    —**Men's Health Magazine**[1]

W e've considered the younger men in their "new normal" and "odyssey" years and we've looked at some of the challenges of postmodernism that may keep a man from the church. But with this brief survey of the clash of traditional and postmodern cultures, what generalizations emerge? What things could we say about men that seem foundational, that will best help us in developing relationships with and among them for Christ?

I believe there are indeed some fairly universal qualities of men today, at least in our Western culture. To understand them is to move a little closer to a welcome-back stance among us leaders. Let's look at some of the internal assumptions within the men who are our "market"—those who inhabit the future church.

Five Unexamined Assumptions in Men's Minds

I'm speaking of conscious or unconscious bits of "self-talk" that influence, motivate and inform their decisions. We could call them myths men tend to believe, false assumptions, or skewed perspectives. These aren't the only ones, of course. But look into your own thinking: do they resonate there?

ASSUMPTION #1: "I became an adult when I left home." Merely renting an apartment, owning a car and getting a job does not make one a man. Yet many younger guys think it's automatic. Nor does having a girlfriend and producing a child make one a father. Rather, character formation is the key. Has one come to a place of *authentic* adult manhood in which he can say (as Robert Lewis suggests): "I have reached a point in life at which I continuously *reject passivity* in my relationships, *accept responsibility* in the larger world, *lead courageously* in my community and focus on the *greater reward* of the heavenly kingdom"?

- *Opportunity for the Mainline Church:* Set up clear pathways for boys to enter forms of initiation into manhood through your church. In some churches this could be tied to the confirmation process, with tracks for boys and girls classes that include mentoring components. Rites of initiation/passage would be clearly defined and young men would be called to experience these rites with their father's central involvement.

Biblical support:

> *When I was a child, I spoke as a child, I understood as a child, I thought as a child; but when I became a man, I put away childish things. For now we see in a mirror, dimly, but then face to face. Now I know in part, but then I shall know just as I also am known.* (1 Corinthians 13:11, 12)

Brad Mogavero's Rite of Passage, June 16, 2012,
Evansville, Indiana

ASSUMPTION #2: "I can engineer my own little world into perfection and peace." Guys are notorious for believing in "life engineering" and many cling to it with fierce determination all their lives. It can go in two directions. First, there's the man who attempts to create a personal utopia through having at least one area of life that is "the best—and flawless". This is the man who thinks, "I will build the most amazing large-screen, hi-def television home theater system, beyond anything in my neighborhood. And when I'm finally enjoying that system—which will be *perfect*—I'll know perfect peace."

So, you want kickin' hi-def entertainment? Just ask Ralph. He'll show you a home entertainment center so packed with state-of-the-art gadgets that a major TV-studio exec would flush with envy. He's wired and programmed it all himself; he's engineered a soundstage Shangri-la, right in his own basement. But better leave him alone down there—and *don't* ever touch the equipment!

There's a second way this can go. This is the man who takes up a strictly problem-solving approach to existence. He believes he can always force things to turn out exactly the way he wants them to be. Bill says to himself, "No matter what happens in life, I'll figure it out and I'll fix it." Problem is, this attitude rarely stays confined to the fixing of his own life. If he's married with children, he'll be the guy who responds to every need with a "just do it this way" word of advice. Many wives and sons and daughters have received all the answers they need for a perfect, peaceful life. But they long to receive a little affection from a critical, problem-solving husband and dad.

- *Opportunity for the Mainline Church:* Demonstrate the pure *grace* of God with practical power. Show men how they can only, ultimately, find perfection and peace in the perfect Prince of Peace, Jesus Christ. That is, present the gospel in a substantial manner that pulls no punches about our sinful sense of self-dependence. We are called to a higher plain—risking it all on the promises of God to meet our every need as we serve

Him. (Note: see the Christian Leadership Concepts curriculum described in appendix A; it's part of A Journey in Disciple Making.)

Naturally, this will be modeled by the mature Christian men in the congregation. In other words, see this as an opportunity to create accountability groups, where men spend time with other men. In this way they "catch" the exchanged life (see Galatians 2:20).

Biblical support:
But what things were gain to me, these I have counted loss for Christ. Yet indeed I also count all things loss for the excellence of the knowledge of Christ Jesus my Lord, for whom I have suffered the loss of all things, and count them as rubbish, that I may gain Christ. (Philippians 3:7, 8)

ASSUMPTION #3: "If I just had more _____ (fill in the blank), I'd be whole." The specter of codependency seems always to hover at the boundaries of a man's horizon. What will give me peace and satisfaction, once and for all? Will I find it in something, some person, some plan, some entity outside of myself? Or will I find it within me—where the Holy Spirit resides and where the kingdom of light has garrisoned in each Christian believer?

They say the "new car smell" lasts only for a couple of months. It will provide some measure of peace and delight for a while. Enjoy! But we men need to be firmly convinced that our fullest and deepest joy can come only from the life of the Lord who indwells us.

• *Opportunity for the Mainline Church:* Call men to a deeper life by modeling the healing power of silence and solitude in the presence of God. Men need to learn that prayer is a daily decision to simply "be" with God for a time, to listen for Him and enjoy His presence. Teach prayer as a powerful way to connect with the Lord and the truest part of ourselves in His presence. We are in Christ and He is in us. When we draw our sustenance from Him, drinking of living waters, we are less tempted to find our soul-nourishment in the next bright, shiny object on the showroom floor.

Biblical support:

Then He said, "Go out, and stand on the mountain before the LORD." And behold, the LORD passed by, and a great and strong wind tore into the mountains and broke the rocks in pieces before the LORD, but the LORD was not in the wind; and after the wind an earthquake, but the LORD was not in the earthquake; and after the earthquake a fire, but the LORD was not in the fire; and after the fire a still small voice. (1 Kings 19:11, 12)

Be still, and know that I am God. (Psalm 46:10)

ASSUMPTION #4: "I can keep my religion at bay." This is the attempt to compartmentalize the spiritual component of one's life. Yet it's impossible. Why? Because we live completely and totally by our religion every day that we draw breath.

Our "religion" is whatever is unconditional for us, whatever is of the highest value, that for which we sacrifice all else. For some men, it is their families; for others, it is their motorcycle. And there are myriad options between the extremes. As theological writer Ronald Rolheiser has pointed out, *our spirituality is what we do with our desire.*[2] All men are involved in the religious pursuit, whether they are conscious of it or not. Our job as leaders is to bring them back to the Source of all spiritual longings.

I think of my friend Andy—41 years old, married with three kids. Listen to his words when I interviewed him for his thoughts on this chapter's theme.

Jay: Where were you, spiritually, six or seven years ago?

Andy: I had a stereotypical idea of home and church— which is that my wife maintains the relationship, continues to want the family to be part of church and I try to be a good husband. Therefore, I went to church basically to keep the peace. But I didn't really have any investment in it emotionally. It was just something we would "do as a family".

Jay: Sounds like you were one of hundreds of thousands of husbands out there whose wives are dragging them to church.

Andy: Well, I was the typical Roman Catholic, I guess, raised with a mom who ran the religious side of our house while my father was uninvolved in that part. He had limited involvement in the church as I was growing up, attending on Sundays. So I guess I figured I could be like Dad and keep "religion" kind of separated off from my real life.

Jay: You wouldn't consider yourself an atheist, exactly, though?

Andy: Actually, I had what I now would call an undefined spiritual belief. I didn't know where it came from, but for me the connection was nature, the outdoors. As a kid I would read stories of Indians and their beliefs and I figured there is a spiritual "presence" in the world, but I never connected it back to the God of the Bible. So the question was—is there a God? I thought there was something; I just didn't know what.

But that was okay. It was enough to just go to church with the family, then forget about it.

The upshot is that Andy was invited to a nonthreatening men's event at my church. He got to know some men he considered "average, normal guys", but who had a deep love for their Savior. They rubbed off on him. To make a long story short, a decade later, Andy and his family are now truly effective evangelists in their community.

• *Opportunity for the Mainline Church:* Make sure you have an intentional Christian formation process for men in your church and be sure that one focus is on *knowing lost men.* Recognize that it typically takes about five years to see the conversion process unfold in a man to the point that a formerly secular guy—with deep spiritual hunger—finally says out loud(!): "I don't know how it happened, exactly, but I guess I really am a Christian now! Yep, I love Jesus." The other focus is something to engender in your entire church congregation: "Around here, it's *belonging before believing.*" Can your church love men into the fellowship, long before those folks know how to worship and believe as you do?

Biblical support:
Then Paul stood in the midst of the Areopagus and said, "Men of Athens, I perceive that in all things you are very religious; for as I was passing through and considering the objects of your worship, I even found an altar with this inscription:

TO THE UNKNOWN GOD

Therefore, the One whom you worship without knowing, Him I proclaim to you . . . for in Him we live and move and have our being, as also some of your own poets have said, 'For we are also His offspring.'" (Acts 17: 22, 23, 28)

ASSUMPTION #5: "I'm just not the emotional type." All of us human beings are the emotional type. The question is, to what extent are we (a) aware of the emotions coursing through us and (b) skilled at channeling them toward productive purposes? For men, the particular challenge is to face the pain of "unpleasant" emotions: sadness over past and current losses or angers and frustrations amidst life's trials that aren't allowed to surface.

Much of the time, men must be "nice" in order to keep the peace at the job or in the home. Many men have buried a lifetime of unacknowledged pain, to the point that they can hardly feel any genuine emotion in any situation.

One of my friends, a pastor, tells about a time when he was riding in the front seat of a hearse, going to the cemetery, where he would preside over the burial service for a 16-year-old girl. In the back seat was the father of the girl. "This man was repeating a phrase, over and over again," says my friend. "I will never forget his words, because they were so deeply sad to me. He kept saying, 'Tell me what to feel; I just don't know what to feel.'"

Why are so many men out of touch with what they actually feel? Let's face it: all of us came up short, to some degree, in terms of our longing for perfect love and acceptance as children. The pain of that loss generates a deep sadness in us that is hard to acknowledge and fearful to touch. We easily try to bury our grief over that hurting child. As psychologist John Bradshaw says, in *Healing the Shame that Binds You*: "It is not the traumas we suffer in childhood which make us emotionally ill, but the inability to express the trauma."[3]

- *Opportunity for the Mainline Church:* Create church settings in which men feel at ease with entering small groups. Many of the groups will be project oriented, but at least one should have a "sharing" focus. In it, men know they can gradually open their hearts to one another in an environment dedicated to confidentiality and mutual support.

STORY FROM THE MISSION FIELD
JAY CROUSE

Many readers will be familiar with gender-specific, small groups from spiritual retreat weekend experiences such as Cursillo, Walk to Emmaus, Tres Dias and others. This small-group experience is intended to develop in us a spiritual discipline of accountability in key areas of our life with three to four trusted fellow Christians.

In 1998, as I was reviewing Pat Morley's very successful men's book, *The Man in the Mirror*, in the appendix, I came across a set of probing questions intended to keep small-group conversation focused and on track. I called Pat and asked him if he would allow me to print these questions on a wallet-size card for easy access. His response was, "Why didn't I think of that!" Today, these cards are referred to as "game plan for gathering" and are available through Men and the Church Ministry.

Being in a weekly, accountability group with three to four other men has been a part of my faith journey since the late 1980s. The benefits are immeasurable. The questions allow me to examine my life on a regular basis. Being with men in this setting allows me to listen, gain wisdom, trust other men, laugh together at life's challenge and learn to be vulnerable and to pursue God in an intentional way.

The challenges of life are too great for men to walk alone. The support and encouragement of a band of brothers can make the difference in a life well lived.

Biblical Support:
> *And lest I should be exalted above measure by the abundance of the revelations, a thorn in the flesh was given to me, a messenger of Satan to buffet me, lest I be exalted above measure. Concerning this*

thing I pleaded with the Lord three times that it might depart from me. And He said to me, "My grace is sufficient for you, for My strength is made perfect in weakness." Therefore most gladly I will rather boast in my infirmities, that the power of Christ may rest upon me. Therefore I take pleasure in infirmities, in reproaches, in needs, in persecutions, in distresses, for Christ's sake. For when I am weak, then I am strong. (2 Corinthians 12:7-10)

It's Time to Welcome Them Back!

In **Part 1** of this book, we've looked at the problem of lost and missing men in our pews and we've tried to get a sense of *who* they are and *what* they think—especially focusing on the younger generations, for obvious reasons. Now, as we enter **Part 2**, it's time to shift focus. Let's consider *how* we are to welcome these men back. That's next.

Your Next-Step Action Plan

TIME FOR STUDY. Do a personal study of the "biblical support" portions of this chapter. Do one per day, for a week. Ask the Lord to give you insight into how these Scriptures should apply to your life personally and to the men's ministry in your church. Then talk it over with another man who is interested in ministry to men.

For Personal Reflection

1. Which of the five *assumptions* seems to ring true in my own life? In what ways?

2. How do I see these assumptions at work in other men? Could I be of help to any of these guys? What are some ways I might prayerfully consider?

3. Think of some of the men in your pews right now. What would help them take a next small step toward discipleship? What is my possible role in this?

4. What ministry event might catch their interest? Why? Who can I talk with about this?

For Group Discussion

1. See if your group can name some younger men in your church and community who seem to need mentoring. How are they expressing their masculinity at the moment? What kinds of reaching out would work with them?

2. Talk together about where you are in the stages of life. What do you see as your most important tasks to accomplish as a man these days? What are the opportunities and challenges before you at the moment?

3. When have you tried to "engineer your own little world into perfection"? How did/is that working for you? Tell a story about it.

4. How can a local men's ministry, especially in your particular denomination, reach out to guys who think, "I can keep my religion at bay"? Come up with some specific ideas in your discussion time.

PART II

A NEW INVITATION:
The Welcomed Man

Chapter 5

Are You Ready to Befriend the Unchurched Man?

The evangelistic harvest is always urgent. The destiny of men and of nations is always being decided. Every generation is strategic. We are not responsible for the past generation, and we cannot bear the full responsibility for the next one; but we do have our generation. God will hold us responsible as to how well we fulfill our responsibilities to this age and take advantage of our opportunities.

Billy Graham[1]

In chapter 1 of this book, I asked, *Leader, are you ready to take up the banner and advance?* Readiness is the key, whether one is poised on the brink of a great charge into the breach or answering yes to the question of men and their future in the church.

At the siege of Badajoz, many were ready to sacrifice everything for the vision of glory that consumed them. In fact, some were even willing to try bribing the higher-ups to

71

be able to lead the charge! Consider two men who aspired to the ranks of the Forlorn Hope.

It was reported from the battlefield that a certain Lieutenant Harvest, having previously been promoted to captain that day, still wanted desperately to volunteer for the Hope that would advance to the castle walls that night. He wanted his honor to be upheld—and it was, though posthumously, on the morning after.

Another soldier on that day, a Major James Singer, is remembered for having said to a friend as the battle approached, "Tomorrow I shall be a lieutenant-colonel or in the kingdom of heaven." The latter was his fate.[2]

I say these things to remind us of the seriousness of the mission before us. This question of the future of the church is indeed a matter of life and death.

Thankfully, the *unchurched* man can quickly become the welcomed man. But we need to be ready with that welcome by preparing ourselves and our churches on several fronts. The chapters ahead will explore five of these areas:

> **Personal:** being able to befriend and invite the lost man (this chapter)
> **Environmental:** pursuing a man-friendly church atmosphere (chapter 6)
> **Structural:** having a system of discipling in place (chapter 7)
> **Relational:** being ready to mentor others into disciple makers (chapters 8 and 9)
> **Pastoral:** standing ready to help the hurting, wounded man (chapter 10)

That's what's ahead. For now, let's begin with our own *personal readiness* for reaching out.

What's Your B.I.O.?

No, I'm not talking about your résumé. I refer to your "befriending and inviting orientation." To be personally ready to welcome men, you'll need to score high on the scale of friendliness and willingness to build relationships/friendships. After all, it is only through relationships with the lost that we will reach them and men are desperate for our friendships.

In his book *Bowling Alone,* Robert Putnam[3] shows that we are becoming increasingly disconnected from family, friends and neighbors. Those brothers, neighbors and coworkers are waiting for you to befriend them—genuinely, sincerely, with no ulterior motive other than your love and concern. My experience is that men are looking for authentic, genuine, fun friendships.

So what are some of the personal qualities that help us befriend and gather men to us—and, consequently, to Jesus? Reflect on these.

- **Approachability**. I can't think of a more important personal quality in a men's leader than this. Frankly, if you are an unapproachable guy, think about whether your spiritual gifts might be used best behind the scenes. It is no dishonor to take an honest inventory and decide, "I'm probably better at working with things than people."

I know several men in my church who love working on the set-up team for major men's events; the physical act of putting up chairs and tables then tearing it all down afterward gives them a sense of tangible accomplishment. They do this work in the name of Jesus and for His glory. They know that interpersonal relating is not their strong suit; they leave the "personal work" to others.

An approachable man is one who simply exudes openness to others. There is nothing fake or disingenuous about him. He's not trying to be friendly. He just is. He is humble. He listens more than he talks. He won't be shocked by anything you tell him about your past life. He is genuinely interested in you and you can feel it, right off the bat.

Just the opposite was described by humorist Garrison Keillor in his *The Book of Guys*.

> **You go to the [men's] lunch and hear a talk about All for Oneness and afterward you confide in a fellow guy that you are going through a hard stretch right now, and he says, "I can sure sympathize, Jim. Listen, let's get together soon and do some bonding. Really."**
>
> **And he checks his watch, glances around for someone else to talk to. *He can't get away from you fast enough.* He goes off and talks to other people and he says, "Look out for Jim. He strikes me as unstable. A liability to the team. How can we ease him out of here?"**[4]

Don't be the men's lunch guy!

- **Admirability.** It's been said that men follow other men whom they respect. They scope out a guy who claims leadership and observe him for a while. Does he walk the talk? Is he a person of integrity? Can he be trusted to follow through on his promises? Can he keep a confidence? All of these ways bring respect and make a man admirable in the eyes of another.

Perhaps at the top of the list in this regard is the question of whether a leader is able to suffer adversity with a calm dignity. The great Bible scholar Brooke Foss Westcott once said, "Great occasions do not make heroes or cowards; they simply unveil them to the eyes of men. Silently and imperceptibly, as we wake or sleep, we grow strong or we grow weak, and at last some crisis shows us what we have become."[5]

The admirable guy is successful in his chosen endeavors. This certainly doesn't mean he has never failed! But he has succeeded in overcoming and moving through life with a confidence in his Lord and a creative approach to the future. In short, he is a strong man of faith. Men will follow that kind of man.

If we hope to exude a confidence and strength that will be rightfully admired, we'll need to remember that our attitude toward the world around us *depends upon what we are ourselves*. If we are selfish, we will be suspicious of others. If we have a generous spirit, we will likely be more trustful. If we're honest with ourselves, we won't assume deceit in others. If we are inclined to be fair, we won't feel that we are being cheated. In a sense, looking at the men around you is like looking in a mirror.

- **Casting Light.** This has to do with the overall "aura" you give off in the world as a Christian. This may seem strange, but I'm speaking of a biblical concept here.

> *For it is the God who commanded light to shine out of darkness, who has shone in our hearts to give the light of the knowledge of the glory of God in the face of Jesus Christ. But we have this treasure in earthen vessels that the excellence of the power may be of God and not of us. We are hard-pressed on every side, yet not crushed; we are perplexed, but not in despair. . .* (2 Corinthians 4:6-8)

Did you notice that something wonderful—the very light of God—shone forth from the face of Jesus? We are to be like him in this.

I relate it to the word *epiphany,* which comes from the Greek word in this text, *epiphanous,* meaning to "shine upon." It has to do with what emanates from your person: is it an encouraging, inviting, open spirit? The man who casts light is unguarded, letting the light of Christ shine through him.

This is not something you could ever manufacture or generate in your own power. It is the giving over of your whole self—body, mind, and spirit—to the influence of the indwelling Christ. In that way He shines through you. Other men see that light and are drawn to it, for they are simply drawn to the beauty of Christ in you.

I think of Moses coming down from the presence of God. His face glowed with the glory. Glory, *kavod* in the original Hebrew text of the Bible, means weightiness, as in a *substantial* person. That is what God can give to any dedicated leader.

Yet just as Moses had spent time in God's presence before he was able to glow with God's life, so we leaders must make sure we are spending time daily with the Light of Life. He can't help but rub off on us and we can't help but reflect His attractiveness to the men around us.

I like how the great Christian educator Henrietta Mears spoke of this: "Are you proving that the Christian life is a joyful, happy thing? Do you look glad that you are a Christian? Does your life radiate joy and enthusiasm? Check yourself carefully on this before you teach it. Make the Christian life contagious."[6]

- **Attentiveness.** If you are an attentive leader of men, then when I'm with you, I feel you are constantly conveying, "Your agenda is my agenda." In other words, you have the ability to focus on me with genuine interest.

Therefore, when reaching out to unchurched men, a key principle in the forefront of your mind will be: "I don't care how much you know until I know how much you care." Men can tell when that is true of you.

Robert Lewis says that in his ministry he always starts with the practical, real-life issues first, then brings in the Bible later. I suggest that this principle holds in our interpersonal relationships with unchurched men too. Be truly interested in that man and his needs. Listen to him without thinking about what you are going to say next. Listen without responding in generalizations. Listen, and ask questions that invite him to go deeper:

"What's happening with you these days, my friend?"
"Tell me a little more about that. . ."

It's tough to overdo it when commending good listening for one who wishes to befriend men for Christ. Evangelism traditionally has been understood as only our words to others. However, it is a new day! The American Baptists and the United Church of Canada have reprinted in their materials some insightful words.

It would be a great thing if Christianity became a listening religion more than a talking religion, if each Christian became a practiced listener rather than a habitual talker. If the church became known as one place where anyone with a burden on his or her heart would be sure to find listening, understanding, and acceptance, that would be quite a reversal or reformation. God gave each of us two ears and only one mouth.[7]

The point is, we need more faith in prevenient grace, as explained by A. W. Tozer in *The Pursuit of God.*

> Christian Theology teaches the doctrine of prevenient grace which briefly stated, means that before a man can seek God, God must first have sought the man. . . .We pursue God because, and only because, He has first put an urge within us that spurs us to the pursuit.[8]

We need to remember that God loves that man standing before us much more than we do. And God has been "working on him" long before we met him (see John 16:8-11). That man may say "yes" or "no" to the convicting ministry of the Holy Spirit that comes through hearing the gospel. But can we trust God with this guy's soul? Yes, because our job is simply to put up no obstacles, to befriend and invite and then leave the converting to the Savior. For Scripture tells us God "is not willing that any person would perish, but that every person would come to conversion" (1 Peter 3:9, AR).

- **Be a blessing-giver.** Does your basic approach to men abound with words and deeds that bless them? Or to put it another way: When a man walks away from a conversation with you, does he feel a little lighter? Is his step a little more confident? Has his outlook on life brightened to some degree?

In their book *The Blessing,* Gary Smalley and John Trent point to the importance of conveying blessing in our relationships (see, for instance, how this plays out in the relationship between David and Jonathan in 1 Samuel 18-20). The authors list five elements of blessing that flow from scriptural foundations.

1. *Meaningful Touch:* being unafraid to give a pat on the back or a warm handshake or hug. (See 2 Samuel 1:23-26; 1 Samuel 20:34-42; Romans 16:16.)
2. *Spoken Words*: being quick to state truthful, genuine and encouraging affirmations. "You must have loved winning that bass-fishing tournament, Dave. What patience!" (See 1 Thessalonians 4:18; 5:11, 14; Romans 4:19; Ephesians 4:32; James 5:16.)
3. *Expressing High Value:* showing that we really believe each man is created in God's image, loved unconditionally by Him and therefore held in high esteem by us. "I'm proud of you and the way you handled that conflict, Jim. You remind me of my high school basketball coach—he never gave up on anybody." (See Mark 1:10-11; Philippians 2:3.)
4. *Picturing a Special Future:* helping a man envision the blessed results of his good choices. "Sam, I see you getting this project together in no time. And you'll love enjoying this deck next summer with your wife and kids." (See Jeremiah 29:11-13; 1 Corinthians 2:7-16.)
5. *An Active Commitment:* loving a guy in *deed* as well as in word. "I never knew plumbing work could be so down and dirty, Phil. But I'm glad I could help out with the digging." [9] (See John 13:4-15; James 2:15-16.)

It's amazing how friendships can develop and deepen when we commit to being a blessing-giver among men. We will come across countless men who are looking for just that kind of encourager.

- **Passion.** No one feels welcomed by the bored and unenthusiastic invitation. . . to join the greatest, most challenging mission in the world! In 1996 I had the high privilege of carrying the Olympic torch through the streets of Sarasota, Florida. I had never known what it felt like to be a hero until that awesome day. For a few hours I was clearly and tangibly a hero in my family and community.

However, an important idea came to me as I ran: although I was holding tight to the torch, it was actually the *flame* that I was moving forward to its destination. That was the important thing, passing the flame to the next runner. Since then, I have been passing this flame—a burning passion for ministry to men—up and down the Florida Gulf Coast and beyond. I am passionate about reaching men and drawing them back into the life of the church. There's no substitute for passion in the leadership of men.

- **Be a Teammate**. If passion is central to welcoming men back to church, it must be the kind that encourages teamwork. A befriending and welcoming men's leader is one who "plays well with others" and gets involved with them in heading where they want to go. Of course, they may need to be helped with seeing where they *really* want to go, but then we get on board and go with them.

It's especially important to be comfortable with giving away power and helping men—even those who aren't yet in the fold—to take ownership of projects. Robert Putnam makes the point that the more a person's activities depend on the actions of others, the greater the dropout rate in participating. This is key for us in reaching men! "What really matters from the point of view of social capital and civic engagement," says Putnam, "is not merely nominal membership, but *active and involved* membership."[10]

The bottom line for the church is this: Get men involved, give them a pivotal role, challenge them with meaningful ministry to do and show them clearly where they are going in the mission.

- **Receptivity.** Remember the men who came to our father Abraham one day as he sat by his tent? We modern readers know a secret about them: they were angels in disguise (see Genesis 18; in fact, one was likely a *theophany*—God in disguise). But the point is, good ole Abe received his guests with the warmest hospitality. Then, in a New Testament reference to this event, we are cautioned: "Do not forget to entertain strangers, for by so doing some people have entertained angels without knowing it" (Hebrews 13:2).

Imagine what it would be like for an unchurched man to walk home from an encounter with you and your church men—maybe from a barbeque or bowling night—and feel *as if he had been received as a possible angel*. He might be thinking things like this:

> They seemed to accept me without question.
> They invited me to join the fun—before they knew my name!
> They never asked me about my beliefs.
> They talked about the next time we'd meet.
> They didn't get all "superior" on me.
> They were so open about their own struggles and problems.
> And. . . they bought my food for me, without explanations.

That kind of radical hospitality is the way of Jesus. Yes, words will come, eventually. But at first, we simply *receive* a new guy. Period. We don't demand any particular response. We don't require any particular belief. "In the end," says Alan Jones, "faith comes not from indoctrination from the outside, but from the Spirit of God bursting out from inside us."[11] We must learn to trust that process with every man.

No one can perfectly embody every one of the character qualities above with perfect consistency. But would you be willing to begin gauging yourself by them? Then ask God to grow you in needed areas. At the same time, work to improve in the areas where you are weak. Do this in action, as you keep working with men. So much of the answer to welcoming them back comes down to your personal ability to convey a compelling invitation.

Will You Tap the Power of P.I.?

Do you tend to see the glass half empty or half full? I'm an optimist on welcoming men back to the church. I believe it can be done and in Spirit-inspired fashion. One reason comes from some of the statistics I've found at www.barna.org. Consider two tidbits.[12]

1. **"The proportion of unchurched men has grown by nine percentage points since 1991. Today an estimated 39% of all men can be deemed unchurched—that is, having not attended a church event, other than a special service such as a wedding or funeral, in the past six months."**
2. **"Despite decreases in core religious behaviors, men are no less likely to read from the Bible these days than they were 20 years ago (41% in 2001, 40% in 1991). In fact, men and women are now equally likely to read the Bible during a typical week."**

Okay, so men are going missing from the church and there has been a downward spiral. But those men are reachable. Many are spiritually seeking. Many have open hearts, as proven by their steady Bible reading habits. This encourages me to renew my strong belief in the power of P.I.: Personal Invitation.

In other words, when we look at welcoming men back to church from a *positive perspective*—looking at the glass half full rather than half empty—we'll remember that 95% of Christian men in America can be found in our local churches. In other words, the men now in our churches have decided to follow Jesus *at one level or another*. They are our disciples. And we should be bustin' it to equip these Christian men to be our front line in an all-out effort to personally invite unchurched men back.

Regardless of the circumstances, the church of Jesus Christ still belongs to Him. So let's get biblical, smart and strategic by renewing Jesus's model of welcoming invitation. What did Jesus do? Here's a typical scene.

> *And Jesus, walking by the Sea of Galilee, saw two brothers, Simon called Peter, and Andrew his brother, casting a net into the sea; for they were fishermen. Then He said to them, "Follow Me, and I will make you fishers of men." They immediately left their nets and followed Him. Going on from there, He saw two other brothers, James the son of Zebedee, and John his brother, in the boat with Zebedee their father, mending their nets. He called them, and immediately they left the boat and their father, and followed Him.* (Matthew 4:18-22)

Our Lord perfectly exemplifies a basic truth: *Men follow men, not programs.* Thus, Jesus called common, regular, everyday men into a great challenge: to fish for other men. Just as many men will do today, if we just get up the courage to invite, they will drop what they are doing and follow Jesus. They can become disciples.

Because Jesus knows the hearts of men, He challenged them. And they loved His challenge so much that most of the 12 who initially responded gave their lives for this Man and His vision—to share the gospel and build the church for Him.

Building my local church has been vital for me for two reasons. First, my ministry to men commitment, from day one, can be found in the book of Matthew.

And I also say to you that you are Peter, and on this rock I will build My church, and the gates of Hades shall not prevail against it. (Matthew 16:18)

Second, it is men in our local churches, where the disciples are, who have decided, at one level or another, to drop their nets and follow Jesus.

Now, I'll close this chapter with a common complaint that I hear about the usefulness of personal invitation. It goes like this: "Jay, I hear what you're saying, but the men in my world want none of it. They are totally independent, self-sufficient and satisfied with their lives, *from all I can see.* Some are even quite adamant about their *not* needing God. And others, to put it plainly, just seem to like sinning—going out with lots of different women and partying. So, I'm not going to get anywhere with any of these guys, no matter how much I try to invite them."

My response? First, "from all I can see" are key words in this man's statement. Most every man is living with some hidden pain around the meaning of his life and legacy. So, here is my suggestion: be patient and keep loving the guy. Be there. Try not to act frustrated with his choices. However, as one young pastor, Peter Haas, put it,

Sinning is a lot like eating chocolate-covered poop. When you become aware that the warm morsel of filth in your mouth was less than satisfying, you're going to need a friend nearby. And I want to be that friend standing with a big bowl of spiritual ice cream or at least some mouthwash. How would you ever find your way to my bowl of ice cream if I motivated you with shame?[13]

Okay, I know it will take you a while to get that image out of your mind! However, Haas makes his point. In the tough cases, where a person is satisfied with his life in the flesh, let him go ahead and enjoy. . . until. The worst thing you can do is judge your friend harshly and cut off his path to God's love. After all, it is the Holy Spirit's role, not ours, to

> . . .*prove to the people of the world that they are wrong about sin and about what is right and about God's judgment.* (John 16:8, GNT)

Don't hijack the role of the Holy Spirit in another guy's life. The primary goal of preaching the gospel is to inspire faith. We do it by taking that first crucial step: making a friend with a potential brother in Christ.

Let's say you've got a handle on what's needed in your personal readiness for reaching out. Is there anything your local church can do to spruce up its masculine welcome mat? We'll dig into this question in our next chapter.

STORY FROM THE MISSION FIELD

DAVID HUNIHAN

I started following Christ before I really had a relationship with Him. My wife, Lauren, and I started going to church regularly after our first child was born, thinking it was the right thing to do. We tried all kinds of churches and finally wound up at one that reminded us both of the churches in which we grew up.

One day, this guy came up to me before the service and invited me to a men's event, which led me to join a small group that met weekly. I met with these men, once a week, for over 12 years. Other men came alongside me and we started learning about the Lord together. We read books and discussed them, like the *Prayer of Jabez*, which was given to me by that same guy who invited me to my first men's event. Then I, in turn, gave *Prayer of Jabez* to about everyone I knew.

Little by little, I was waking up and getting to know God. I had always believed in Him, but I didn't really *know* Him. Then a miraculous thing happened. A friend of mine in my small group gave me a Men's Devotional Bible that had a reading plan in the back for reading the Bible through in a year. So in 2000, Lauren and I decided to read the Bible together, cover to cover. I had read the Bible in college, more as a textbook, and picked it up now and again, but it is a whole different experience reading it from beginning to end.

Passion ignited in me. I realized how little I knew; how involved God really is in our lives; how much he wants to be a part of everything we do and how much He longs for His lost children. In the space of that year, I left the company I had been working for and started my own business, which I dedicated to the Lord.

I set about learning all I could about God and His Son Jesus Christ. I read books and listened to sermons on the radio from the likes of David Jeremiah, Chip Ingram, John Bevere, Philip Yancey, Lee Strobel, Charles Stanley, and Ravi Zacharias, just to name a few. I thought I had to have all the answers to be able to respond to every question someone had about Jesus. I thought if I knew all the arguments, then I could convince everyone around me to believe. I am sure I seemed pretty obnoxious at that point and probably turned quite a few people off.

Around that time, I met Jerry Smith, one of the instructors for Equipping the 70. He taught me an incredibly valuable lesson. After I expressed my frustration at not being able to learn all the counterarguments to convince nonbelievers, he said to me "David, you have it all wrong. You are called to be the **witness**. What do witnesses do? They come, give their testimony and that is all. They aren't the judge, the jury, or the prosecuting attorney. And you can't dispute someone's testimony, because it's what they believe. And if they live it out in their lives, it becomes truly powerful. Be the witness."

How often do we tell others about a restaurant or a movie we like, but we won't tell them, or better yet show them, about the way to eternal life? Well, that one encounter with Jerry Smith changed everything for me. I knew I had to tell people about Jesus. I knew I had to be a "witness".

From that point on, as St. Francis of Assisi said, I was going to preach the gospel at all times, and, when necessary, I would use words. I would read and study, first and foremost the Bible, but also books about discipleship, such as Phil Downer's *Eternal Impact*, which taught me about multiplication and about *Operation Timothy,* an investigative Bible Study for Christian businessmen.

But most important, I started to live my life out as a Christian, careful in word, thought and deed. And at work, it got noticed. My employees saw a difference and held me accountable. Unfortunately, my business failed and people continued to watch me. I had no idea how many people were waiting to see how I would handle it. And even though the business failed, God didn't let me stumble. He would continue to use me, simply on a new path.

My failure turned into a positive witness for the Lord. I met an atheist at my new job. He had been inoculated against Jesus by other Christian business owners who were bad "witnesses". But he saw that Lauren and I were different.

As we got to know Roger, we appealed to his intellect, began to talk about God and encouraged him to read some books. Eventually he was open to exploring Operation Timothy together, so we began meeting weekly to go through the workbooks, answer and discuss his questions, and eventually read through the Bible. Six short months later, Roger came to Christ.

Before I agreed to meet with him, I told him I would commit the time if he would do two things with me. First, he had to commit to finish the first workbook and make our regular weekly meetings. Second, he had to agree to do the same for someone else, if things turned out the way I believed they would.

So Roger, a former atheist, is now looking to multiply the kingdom of God. . . all because a man named Jay Crouse put his arm around me and invited me to a men's steak night at his church.

I thank God for that.

Your Next-Step Action Plan

CONSIDER YOUR READINESS TO WELCOME. Go back and study the five "elements of blessing" from the Scriptures. Read the Bible passages listed and consider their application to the ways you relate to others. What man in your world could be encouraged by your blessing him in one of these ways? Make a solid plan to contact this one man this week!

For Personal Reflection

1. How do I assess my *personal* readiness for reaching out to men who need Christ?

2. What is my B.I.O. (Befriending and Inviting Orientation)? What things could I do to improve my "score"?

3. When have I seen the power of personal invitation at work? What is this telling me regarding my approach in men's ministry?

4. Study the fruit of the Spirit listed in Galatians 5:22, 23. Do a personal inventory (with an accountability partner, if possible) of your own character in regard to these fruits that should be growing in every Christian man.

For Group Discussion

1. Share together some personal stories about how you each assess your B.I.O. effectiveness in the six areas listed in this chapter.

2. What is your experience with "casting light", of "approachableness" and of being a "blessing-giver"?

3. To what extent does our ability to "make friends" determine the effectiveness of a men's ministry? Give some examples to support your response.

4. "Men follow men, not programs." Do you agree or disagree? Why or why not?

5. "Don't hijack the role of the Holy Spirit in another man's life." What does this statement inspire in us?

Chapter 6

Can You Man Up Your Church?

A man achieves world domination every time he does something awfully well. A guy who has a good fastball, or knows physics like his own backyard, or can pick up a .22 and pick off a pine cone at a hundred yards knows this. Guys need this feeling if they're going to survive. . . .We have to be Number 1—sometime, somewhere, if only for ten minutes—or else we sag inside and become sad and careful, a guy who, when he stands up, you hear the tinkle of broken dreams.

—Garrison Keillor[1]

Maybe you've heard the story of Ernest Shackleton, the man who set out to explore Antarctica in the early 1900s. He hoped to find the South Pole and his supposed want-ad is a famous bit of lore.

<u>NOTICE</u>

**Men wanted for hazardous journey.
Small wages. Bitter cold.
Long months of complete darkness.**

**Constant danger. Safe return doubtful.
Honour and recognition in case of success.**

It's said that some 5,000 men applied for the 26-man expedition. Shackleton's ad appears on countless posters and tee-shirts in our day, but whether he ever wrote it, no one knows for sure. However, here's my point: Isn't there something about us men that *wants* it to be true? We dream of joining a heroic endeavor and achieving something that truly matters. And once we're convinced of its value, we're willing to pay the price.

If I could sum up the key point I want to make about being ready for men in your local church, I'd say it like this: *Give them what they want in the context of what they need.*

They *want* to be challenged. They *need* the One who challenges them.

A church that's attractive to men knows its primary purpose is not to help them on *their journey* to emotionally satisfying self-development. Rather, men in your church will thankfully respond when they're called to join in *God's journey* of transformational reconciliation:

> *For I consider that the sufferings of this present time are not worthy to be compared with the glory which shall be revealed in us. . .because the creation itself also will be delivered from the bondage of corruption into the glorious liberty of the children of God. . .*
>
> *Who shall separate us from the love of Christ? Shall tribulation, or distress, or persecution, or famine, or nakedness, or peril, or sword?*
>
> *. . .Yet in all these things we are more than conquerors through Him who loved us. . .*
>
> *Now all things are of God, who has reconciled us to Himself through Jesus Christ, and has given us the*

ministry of reconciliation. (Romans 8:18, 21, 35, 37; 2 Corinthians 5:18)

Shades of Shackleton? Could there be any bigger expedition? Let's look closer at three ways you can encourage an *adventure atmosphere* in your congregation.

Make Your Expectations Clear

Do men—even visitors—immediately pick up on "what we mean by *a Christian man* around here"? And do they know what's expected of them in spiritual growth? In practical terms, this might mean such things as these:

- When I hear announcements in church, there are calls to both knitting circles and fishing trips; volunteers needed for hosting the English Tea and also for coaching peewee football.
- I sense that men here care that things are done right. There is nothing slipshod about the buildings and landscaping.
- I leave services with a clear call to action; I know exactly how I could take a first step.
- There is a critical mass of spiritually mature men in this church with whom I would like to hang out—and even follow.
- There is an engaging, well-thought-out process for me to be formed into a mature, Christian man; it's easily accessible to me.
- I identify with the pastor's way of life. I hear about his/ her adventures and I can admire them in many ways.
- I notice that some of the children's Sunday school classes are taught by. . . men!
- I haven't wasted my time in coming to an event, class, or worship. Things move along with orderly

93

flow, showing conscientious planning, with content that is meaningful to me.

- If I want to sing along, I find the key in my range and I'm not repeating "lovely baby Jesus" stuff.
- Prayers are sincere, flow from the heart and show reverence for a God who is bigger than a "buddy" of mine.
- In a church of high liturgy, I hear full-throated responses from male voices. I see kneeling, genu-flecting, crossing done with fervency—men clearly revering their King.
- No one is making me give them a hug, yet I feel a sense of friendliness.

You get the point. A man can enter this local church environment and quickly discern the "steps" that will take him deeper into Christian growth. If he gets involved in a couples' study on marriage for six weeks, he learns that he's expected to (a) apply those principles he's studied, (b) join a group in which he is to some degree accountable and (c) know what next class or event is on the horizon that will take him further along on the journey.

The Barna Group's *State of the Church & Family* power-fully supports the "clear expectations" mandate for dads who are raising families. Consider these intriguing statements flowing from their polling research.

Many churches seem to be remiss in effectively communicating to parents what they expect. Among those who had experience with a church in the last two years as a family, less than half (45%) said the church was "very clear" about what they expected of parents. Among the unchurched parents with recent experience at a church, only one-quarter (27%) said the expectations of the church's leaders were made clear to them.

What it means: When no one is clear about expectations—neither parents nor church leaders—it is difficult for anyone to experience healthy outcomes—families or congregations. One of the implications of this research is that people do not generally look at "the church" itself as the answer to their parenting problems or family crises. In other words, the church feels like a generic solution when most people are facing specific problems.[2]

Such statistics have a decided impact on men, in particular. Men aren't typically into "generic solutions" and they certainly don't want to spend their precious time trying to figure out the mission and purpose of your church. Maybe we have it backwards: are we calling men back to the church, or should we be calling the church back to men?

My point is simply this: we need to offer a compelling vision and strategy if we are to be ready to welcome men back to the church. In my diocese, our strategic planning consultant, Ibby Whitten, asked, "What makes spiritual-growth ministries effective?" Here are her observations, taken from an analysis of cases.

- **They offer small, peer-group interactions.**
- **They offer service opportunities that have meaning for individuals (volunteer, outreach, worship).**
- **They offer comprehensive men's Christian formation opportunities as part of their adult programming.**
- **They offer comprehensive, men's opportunities for evangelism—whether it's asking a fellow parishioner to join the group on occasion or reaching for new members by keeping an "empty**

chair" in the groups—a chair that each member is trying to fill with a new Christian.

Men's ministry leaders, take these findings to heart. Your church needs to offer a mission that matters. Make its discipleship expectations and strategies clear and show men where they're going on the adventure. As David Murrow puts it, "We have asked men to follow our teaching, methods, theology. Men do not follow these things. *Men follow men who are leading them somewhere.*"[3]

Adjust the R.Q. as You Go

I refer here to the Risk Quotient. It's a guy thing. I want to know that my church is calling me to something for which I could lay down my life. It will pervade the atmosphere.

If women are looking for a satisfying *relationship* with God, men long for a satisfying *mission* with God. And any mission of worth is going to involve some risk. When the atmosphere exudes intimacy with Jesus as the prime value, then the gender gap will widen—fatally. After all, a guy is instantly uncomfortable with the word "intimacy"—in church, no less!

So we must recapture the *challenge* of following Jesus. Set high standards; ask much of members. Cool the air a bit and move the thermostat from security to challenge. We need both feminine spirit-harmony, cooperation, nurture and masculine spirit-competition, achievement, victory.

DO set high expectations for Christian growth.
DO replace an academic teaching model with a discipleship training model.
DO show men how tasks and ministries *produce something:* converts and Christ-followers.
DO employ men in service projects for practical witness of Christ's love.

DO charge men a modest amount of money for classes and events, which equates them with value. (Scholarships are always offered.)

DON'T invite men into experiences in which they'll lack competence and confidence.

DON'T give up on moral absolutes in teaching and preaching.

DON'T freeze out unconverted men; invite their talents, even *before* they are in Christ.

DON'T call for supporting an institution above changing the world.

Adjusting the Risk Quotient means keeping an eye on the environment in your congregation and tweaking it where and when you can. You'll be asking: *What is the pulse rate here? Is there any adrenaline flowing at the moment? Is it too easy to follow Jesus from this outpost of the kingdom?* Jesus Himself set the bar high. If a man had courage, he could join the mission.

> *Now it happened as they journeyed on the road, that someone said to Him, "Lord, I will follow You wherever You go."*
>
> *And Jesus said to him, "Foxes have holes and birds of the air have nests, but the Son of Man has nowhere to lay His head."*
>
> *Then He said to another, "Follow Me."*
>
> *But he said, "Lord, let me first go and bury my father."*
>
> *Jesus said to him, "Let the dead bury their own dead, but you go and preach the kingdom of God."*
>
> *And another also said, "Lord, I will follow You, but let me first go and bid them farewell who are at my house."*

> *But Jesus said to him, "No one, having put his hand to the plow, and looking back, is fit for the kingdom of God."* (Luke 9:57-62)

A friend of mine, Allen, who is trying to write a novel, quotes the great novelist Robert Penn Warren with something that applies directly to my theme here: "To put it bluntly: no conflict, no story. If we do find a totally satisfactory adjustment in life, we tend to sink into the drowse of the accustomed. Only when our surroundings—or we ourselves—become problematic again do we wake up and feel the surge of energy, which is life. And life more abundantly lived is what we seek."[4]

As he struggled with his novel's purpose and direction, Allen began reevaluating what he really felt about his own life and its purpose so far. "I was 35 years old and a Christian," he told me. "But I really hadn't stepped back to assess the landscape of my life so far and consider what it meant for my future." He ended up journaling some "this is what I believe so far" statements. Here are the first few that he shared with me.

- **Work, money, possessions are *means* only and never will satisfy the longing for *ends*. They are meant to aid living, but never can they become a satisfying life itself.**
- **The fullest life is a life of faith, which by definition, means a life of *risk*. To cease risking, or to run from it, is to die, little by little, inside. To engage the riskiness of life is to call out to God. It is the place of prayer. The *point of decision* is the meeting place that God has chosen. *We* will decide, at that point, whether to see His face in our lives.**

Don't these themes, at some level, resonate deep within the heart of every man? Can we reach into that place and meet them there in our churches?

Motivate for Difference Making

One pastor I know, Becky Robbins-Penniman of Church of the Good Shepherd, in Dunedin, Florida, offered a powerful sermon to her congregation on Father's Day. She spoke primarily to the men. When I asked for a copy of her sermon and read it through, I wanted to make a movie of it – or light it up for display on the Goodyear blimp at the Super Bowl! In other words, I was inspired! Listen to her words:

> The irony is that the Western church we now have is the product of men who built it up for nearly two thousand years. And now, the men don't actually like the church they built. As a consequence, for the past 40-50 years, the church has been dying, not growing.
>
> I'm not about to get into any huge discussion about what happened next. It really doesn't matter. What matters is what comes next. What would it take for the church to be a place guys want to be?
>
> Here's what I see: in our Western culture, men have instilled in them, from a very young age, that the mark of a man is to make a difference, to leave the world a different place because they have lived and acted. It needn't be huge – and rarely is, but it must be something.
>
> Evidently, what has happened in the church for the last 40 years or so is that an increasing number of men have not found the church to be a place that empowers them to make a difference in the world, unless they are in the official leadership ranks.

So, what kind of church environment nourishes that difference-making quality?

- *It's becoming a less-knowing church.* We men's leaders and emerging leaders need to evaluate the church's ministries based on a crucial distinction: "Knowing *about* God" versus "Having an adventure *with* God." We need both, of course, but the call of preaching has traditionally been this: *You must become more* **like** *God!* Though it's true that we are indeed becoming more and more like Christ, that work is for the Holy Spirit to do in us. While the Spirit is working, perhaps our preaching theme ought to be: *Let us walk closer* **with** *God!*

In stressing the need to become holy like God, we have made the focus of our ministries the teaching about God's Word, God's nature, God's will and so on. But if we were to switch to the God-adventure mode, wouldn't we have a more powerful and compelling message—and no doubt a more biblical one, too?

I think of King David, the man after God's own heart. It was David's walk with God, from a young man, that endeared him to the heart of God, in spite of his monumental lapses in holiness.

Pastor Michael Slaughter, in his book *UnLearning Church,* speaks of a church focused less on academics and more on experience.

Marketing gurus understand that today's culture isn't looking for information about products. Just how much could you write down about a Nike shoe after watching one television ad about it? Today's culture isn't looking to understand. Nike commercials don't talk about or even show athletic apparel.

> **Instead, they offer a thirty-second experience. The church could learn something from Nike. People don't want information about your religion—what people really want is a life-altering experience.**
>
> **For any organization to have an impact, it needs a radical product, and the church's radical product is revolutionary people—real followers of Jesus Christ. As churches take seriously Jesus's call to discipleship, they change from consumers to missional movements of God who demonstrate both personal and social holiness.[5]**

If my pastor were Michael Slaughter, I'd be hearing sermons that call me to a radical commitment to Christ and I'd probably be allowed to "talk back" in some kind of sermon forum, too. I'd relish the chance to get onboard with the mission—and I wouldn't assume that I still needed to *know* more before volunteering. I'd only be aware that any hands-on *training* I needed was instantly available.

- *It's creating less-cloistered Christians.* Some pastors and church leaders have made a radical decision. They are no longer going to make the long-term members the ones at the top of their list of folks they hope to please in worship. They've decided just the opposite. They tell their members that they have no right to seek their own pleasure or to "get something out of the service" for themselves. It's great when that happens, but it's not the purpose of what the church does.

Rather, as Pastor Peter Haas says, "We tell our people: 'Nobody gets what they want on Sunday mornings except the one lost sheep that heaven wants to rejoice over.' Point: A church that is obsessed with giving, not receiving."[6]

This attitude begins producing an outward-looking, missional church in which Christians no longer see themselves cloistering within the walls with hatches battened against the world. When a man walks into such a church, he'll see lots of extremely messed-up people here. Is that a bad thing?

"Christians who aren't regularly exposed to the messy lives of drug addicts, cohabitating couples and the like," says Haas, "lose their ability to see God's purpose for His church."

Cloistered Christians critique everything based on what's in it for them; they are self-oriented. The adventure-oriented Christian man is different. He's been invited to a welcoming church, one that gives him a mission to engage, one that helps him walk closer to God and one where he sees other men taking up the challenge at every level of life.

Promote a More Masculine Atmosphere!

Do you have a basic grasp of a "masculine atmosphere" concept? Start by getting a handle on these six general principles. . .

1. **Men equate personal distance with safety and security.**
2. **Men communicate through questions.**
3. **Most men are goal or challenge-oriented.**
4. **Men tend to focus and compartmentalize.**
5. **Men choose rules over relationships.**
6. **Men hesitate to express emotion.**[7]

Men's leaders, building relationships is crucial and essential. However, to welcome the unchurched men back, we begin with a welcoming *leader* and a welcoming *atmosphere*. Next, we'll want to have a clear welcoming *structure*—a discernible system—in place for inviting men to become disciples of Jesus. That's what we'll take up in the next chapter.

STORY FROM THE MISSION FIELD

PETE ALWINSON

Immediately after the church service where I was introduced as the possible planter of a new church to be launched in the northeast side of Orlando, three men came up to speak with me. One, a retired engineer with a head full of gray hair said, "I'm going to join your church." The second was a young, unmarried guy sporting a few days' growth on his face, wearing motorcycle boots and leather jacket and holding a helmet in his hand. He said, "I want to talk to you about this church. Can we meet?" Another young man with glasses, who looked more studious than the biker, told me he wanted to talk about my vision for the church. An old guy, a biker and an intellectual. What do I remember from that night? Even though I had just preached the worst sermon ever in my life, because I was so nervous, the Lord had given me three solid contacts for a new church, should I be called. Men—three men. I was incredibly encouraged because I knew with men on board, the church could become a reality.

Twenty-five years later, the church *is* a reality, with over 700 worshipping each week and a full, comprehensive ministry, missionaries and even a preschool. It started with a focus on building men. Those three men were the core of a Bible Study I started on Tuesday mornings, which became our liftoff. The funny thing is that all three of them were engineers and really smart guys and each in his own way contributed to the future health of this church I was blessed to serve for those 25 years.

Why was I motivated to build into men as a part of my top five priorities as a pastor? Just as Adam was called to lead the human race, men were the first priests in Israel and men are called to be the spiritual leaders in the home (Deut. 6), they are also called to be leaders in the church. My somewhat politically incorrect mantra has become, *"As the men of the church goes, so goes the church. A church never gets beyond the quality level of its men."* This is not because men are superior to women. It's simply because God has called men to lead and when they lead well, God's people, His kingdom and His church prospers. Discipling men is God's way to fulfill God's purposes. My own lack of being fathered well by my earthly father has led me on a journey to experience God as my Father and to help other men experience Him as their Father, as well. After all, Jesus taught us to pray, "Our Father. . ."

What happened in our church as a result of this focus? Men felt that they were welcomed at our church. Women felt welcomed too, but men knew I was for them. I hung out with the guys on Wednesday evenings for Bible studies; my officer training class was not just to transfer biblical doctrine, but also to build a relationship with them and build men as family leaders, workers and servant leaders in the church. The men came to see their strength as given to them by God to serve—in the nursery, in children's and youth ministry, in supporting women's ministries, in maintaining the church facilities, in bringing lower income people to the church for meals, in bringing other guys together in adventure trips, in doing evangelism, in supporting other guys in their battle against addictions. One time I asked a parishioner how she and her family had started attending our church. She said, "Well,

I wanted to go to another church, but my husband likes it here." Fine with me.

Did I ever get any push back from being a disciple of men and creating a culture that was pro-men as well as pro-women and children? Some, yes. But leaders are supposed to do what is right, not what is comfortable. The outcome is that the church is still there without me leading it, serving the King every day. The new pastor came into a church with a ton of strong men. It's not a perfect church, but it's a growing church, undergirded by disciples of Jesus who are following hard after Him.

Dr. Pete Alwinson is Vice-President of Leadership and Men's Discipleship, Key Life Network, www.FreedomsEdge.org.

Your Next-Step Action Plan

TAKE THE "GUY FRIENDLY" TEST WITH YOUR MEN. See men's ministry writer David Murrow's test at churchformen. com/wpcontent/uploads/2010/03/Guy_Friendly_Test.pdf.

The test asks 50 questions about the atmosphere of your church. The higher the score, the more likely your church is to appeal to men, though David says, "Not all men are alike."

For Personal Reflection

1. Garrison Keillor, in the opening quotation in this chapter, speaks of men and their need to be excellent at something. What is my own area of skill or expertise? Is there a way for me to express this within my church community?

2. Do I know what is expected of me at my church? Do I have a clear sense of the "route to spiritual growth" for men here?

3. What is the Risk Quotient in my church? How can I tell?

4. Looking again at the "six general principles" of masculine atmosphere that appear at the end of this chapter, where is my church in its level of awareness of these?

For Group Discussion

1. How does the story of Ernest Shackleton strike you? Discuss it!

2. Talk together about the *atmosphere* of your local church. Refer to the bulleted list under the subheading, "Make Your Expectations Clear".

3. Think about the idea of "motivating for difference making." Talk about times when you've experienced this through your church and/or men's ministry.

4. Discuss the practical implications for your church, if you were to become (1) a less-knowing church and (2) less-cloistered Christians.

Chapter 7

Do You Have a Structure in Place?

> *In the business world, we have the saying "Your system is perfectly designed to produce the result you're getting." If you manufacture cars and every third car rolls off the assembly line missing a front right fender, then your system is perfectly destined to produce that result. The same principle applies to our ministries.*
>
> **—Pat Morley,** *No Man Left Behind* [1]

If we're going to welcome men back into the church, we'll need a men's ministry infrastructure ready for them. My inspiration comes from the initial verses of John 15, where Jesus teaches about the vine and branches.

> **"I am the true vine, and my Father is the gardener. . . .you are the branches. If you remain in me and I in you, you will bear much fruit; apart from me you can do nothing."**

Let's think about how a vineyard works. A vine grows up and from it springs branches. Now, the nature of the vine is to grow upward like a tree. But the branches must be supported with an infrastructure—trellis work—that holds them up so they can produce. Without infrastructure, the branches trail the ground and root there, apart from the vine. When that happens, they bear no fruit.

In many of our congregations, the upholding infrastructure just isn't there. When men enter many of our churches, they find myriad undifferentiated priorities and activities. Consequently, they root themselves in the unproductive soil of independence from the *person* of Christ and they separate themselves from the *community* Christ has called them to embrace.

Even more concerning is that our system, with its undifferentiated priorities, forces our churches to what I call *the default mode for men*: having one monthly breakfast (or prayer group, or study, etc.), with the pastor feeling satisfied that "we have something for the men, too." It is a perfectly designed system for producing. . . mediocrity.

Here's a Successful, Time-tested System

With a structure in place, men get the support they need. Then the Gardener can prune them and help them bear fruit.

My friend Pat Morley has graciously allowed me to use and recommend his men's ministry model with churches of southwest Florida. It's an awesome system and I recommend that you run out and buy his book *No Man Left Behind* right now! It explains the model in detail. But for our purposes, here are the highpoints in a nutshell.

- Develop a **Portal Priority**: Have a key purpose for your ministry: namely, making disciples who disciple others (see 2 Timothy 2:2). This ties together all the undifferentiated activities under one purpose, with regard to every man in your church.

- Heighten the **Man Code:** Do what you can to help the atmosphere of the church move to a challenging mission orientation.
- Gather your **three strands of leadership**: a pastor, a key champion layman and a team of allies.
- **Create** a vision for the ministry based on Christ's call to men and then offer **events/activities** that engage the **five types of men**, coming up in this chapter.
- **Capture** the vision by always showing a man the **next right step** after he's been involved in an event or activity.
- **Sustain** the vision by getting men into the Bible so they'll **make disciple makers out of new disciples.** In this way the process starts again, with new men who need Christ entering this disciple making system.

I've tweaked and modified this model for use in my own church and other churches have taken the model and considered how to apply it to their unique situations. The point is that it is a basic infrastructure, something that is crucial and must be in place.

Since this book is about the ways we can intentionally reposition our welcome-back mat—personally, environmentally, structurally, relationally and pastorally—I'm going to lay out six simple steps for you, drawing upon Morley's roadmap as needed. In other words, I want this information to be clear and compact at the moment so that you, a church leader or emerging leader, quickly get the picture of what's needed structurally. Just remember that all of this takes patience and much prayer. Plan on three to five years to get a healthy ministry to men off the ground, but don't make any "system" your key focus. Jesus is your key focus; if He is in it, you will succeed.

Are you ready to begin?

Step 1: Start with Your Pastor

Your ministry to men must start with your pastor's buy-in. I have to admit, though, sometimes I wonder where the clerical passion went! What's holding so many pastors back from enthusiastically embracing the possibilities?

TIME OUT (as I speak to pastors). . .

When I interview pastors and priests about the priority of ministry to men, I receive some interesting feedback! If you are a pastor—or a lay leader interested in how they think—take a moment now to turn to **Appendix B**. There you'll see some pastoral objections, concerns and worries and how I tend to respond.

Time In

Some pastors wonder, "Where, exactly, is this thing headed? Will it move us off of our church's direction?"

Here's one way to approach it. If your direction *isn't* focused on Matthew 28—winning people to Christ and helping them become committed Christ-followers who win others—well, men's ministry might help you get back on track! Seriously, the men will be a great support for any church's serious attempt to fulfill the Great Commission in its local community.

"Pastors are at once excited and nervous," says Steve Sonderman. "They're happy that someone else is grabbing hold of a ministry, but . . . [they] look at the big picture and wonder what additional demands they will face to keep one more ministry going."[2]

Furthermore, pastors may wonder whether the "sales pitch" they're hearing is another way of saying, "Pastor, why aren't you doing a better job around here?"

I sympathize with you pastors. I really do! These are real, heartfelt concerns and I have no desire to belittle them. I simply want you to consider the spectacular "health benefits" that can come to you and your church when men are reached for Christ.

- **Men take an action-oriented approach to ministry, with less risk aversion:**
  "Let's get 'er done" is the mentality.
- **Men will likely bring their families with them to church (whereas many women have to leave hubby home).**
- **Men, when inspired by the mission, have the financial resources to contribute; they bring increased giving.**
- **Men bring a problem-solving practicality to the obstacles and barriers in any ministry.**
- **Men will stand by their convictions, come hell or high water, once they're convinced of value and significance.**

While men are good for the church, this springs from the fact that church is good for men. So let's close this circle. Statistical studies have found that the presence of "involved men" in a congregation correlates with numerical growth and a lessening of conflict among members.[3] In John 4:46-53, the impact a man's faith can have on his family is revealed: when a father came to faith in Jesus, "he *and his whole household* believed." In fact, today, in 93% of households where the father is spiritually focused, the household models that spiritual life.

So, pastor, imagine having **whole households as evangelistic centers** in your church's geographical area. If men lead Christian homes in their neighborhoods—making those homes lighthouses of loving service and witness among their neighbors—they will be bringing new seekers into your church.

Lay leader, remember this: Your passion for men should be a relief and an encouragement to the clergy. This is not a ministry to be laid at the feet of pastors for them to implement. **If an enthusiastic lay leader has been identified, the pastor will naturally move to a supporting role.**

So how do you approach your pastor about ministry to men? Gently, wisely, patiently and prayerfully. Perhaps the best approach is simply to make an appointment, share your vision based on Scripture and show your pastor how your dream fits perfectly with and supports the congregation's mission. Here are some quick, practical pointers for your meeting:

- **Go to the meeting with someone your pastor knows well and trusts.**
- **Go with an attitude of serving and meeting needs. After listening to the pastor, as appropriate, discuss how men's ministry might contribute to church health and growth.**
- **Don't ask the pastor to take on any responsibilities; show how you will be recruiting a team, providing training, arranging events, follow-up, etc.**
- **If appropriate, ask if the pastor might want to participate in a group or be a resource person for leading, teaching, etc.**
- **Have a good, detailed understanding of the church's overall budget and be ready to explain how you will fund the ministry self-sufficiently.**

- **Brainstorm together about potential problems, conflicts, etc.**
- **When appropriate, study the church calendar together and consider good seasons for major events or weekly meetings, etc.**
- **Show that a key component of men's ministry is support for church leaders through prayer, personal encouragement and public loyalty.**

A key to your meeting with any church leader is to avoid asking for resources as your primary pitch. Rather, as you begin discipling one or two other men, start reporting your successes along the way. Show results of any initial efforts you're already involved in. These speak like nothing else.

Step 2: Begin Building Your Team

Start with the three key members of a men's ministry team: the senior pastor, a primary lay champion and a team of leaders to support him. Added to this are the invaluable allies Pat Morley encourages leaders to seek. "Allies are advocates of your disciple-making efforts. Increase the number of allies every year and you will have a vibrant, sustainable ministry to men."[4]

As you consider recruiting your potential team members, remember that you are not hoping to gather a bunch of guys who will do all the work. What you're really doing is gathering a "shepherding board" of men who envision, pray, gather and equip others for the work of the ministry. You are, in short, gathering your spiritual leadership, whose intent is to make disciple makers out of others.

Before going on, I want to make a very important clarification which must permeate throughout your team and men's ministry: we are engaged in a highly relational endeavor. It is man-to-man, networking, 2 by 2, and making connections. The relational call must be at the core of all of your activities. All of them!

Relationships are the heart and soul of ministry to men – relationships with your family, clergy, men of your congregation and community, and most important of all, your relationship with Jesus Christ. Your personal spiritual walk must be strong, vibrant and attractive to others. Regardless of the level of your participation in other aspects of the ministry, this is the most important relationship upon which to focus and fully embrace.

Why is this so? First, because men's spiritual lives and their relationship with Christ is your purpose. To be authentic in this ministry, you must begin with an authentic spiritual life in your own heart.

Second, an authentic relationship with Christ is crucial because the men of your church will quickly assess whether or not you are "walking the talk". When you give your life to Christ, He will work through you to impact *your family first and foremost,* then your church and community. Whether you like it or not, men will notice what is happening in your marriage and family. That is where they will see who you really are—and decide whether you are someone they would like to follow.

How do you go about gathering the team? First, identify a potential champion, a man with passion for this ministry. Let's assume that is you!

Then enlist five to eight men to be on your team and invite each man to be responsible for one focus area of the men's ministry program. Remember the leadership team is not a task force. Its real task is to expand the number of men who are inspired to take up roles in the ministry.

In your initial outreach to gather a team, you can choose either the scattershot approach (larger church) or the personal-contact approach (smaller church).

Big to Small: Send out an invitation to every man with the idea of coming to an informational meeting. They can send back an enclosed postcard, RSVP. Promise food and an interesting presentation. Don't ask for a commitment of any kind, but invite men to consider and pray about potential involvement. For those who express interest, clearly show them the next step.

Small to Big: Personally put together a list of men in your congregation who should be invited to be on your leadership team—five to ten men you've observed who might be able to serve as a beginning leadership team to develop and sustain your ministry. Contact them personally. Ask them to go to lunch and just ask for feedback about your vision for men's ministry. Share your vision, passion and a brief overview of the purpose and goals (conversion and disciple making) of a potential ministry.

Then just listen. Do not ask for any commitment. If a man is not interested, let him know that you will remain interested in him and his life. If he does show interest, invite him to come and observe a leadership team meeting. In any event, keep making friends and building trust. No high pressure.

Once you get a commitment of this small group, recruitment will be a main task over the years. Consider this plan.

> **Let's say you have four committed men on your leadership team. Make a covenant with each other to take one man to coffee or lunch each month and share why discipling men is important to you. . . Follow this process for a year. Assuming each of you misses a month here or there, you will have conversations with at least 40 men. Your passion will not mean much to many of these men. Others will be glad for you, but too busy to get involved themselves. But if just two out of every ten men express an interest in sitting in on a meeting (that**

means eight of your 40 men), and half of those decide to get involved, you will have doubled the size of your leadership team in just a year![5]

No matter the size of your team, remember that you must continue to pastor this group. Make sure they are getting the encouragement and spiritual development they need to be ministers in your church. Pray for them regularly and make sure you pray *with* them. Keep casting the vision before them. In short, these are your disciples. Pour yourself into them.

STORY FROM THE MISSION FIELD

DON INGLE

When my senior pastor tapped me to lead the men's ministry at First Baptist Church Naples, two key elements of infrastructure were already in place. The first was his full support for men's ministry. The second was an existing meeting time for men on a weekly basis: Wednesday evenings from 6:30–8:00 p.m. Men's ministry is much more than a weekly meeting for studying the Word and fellowshipping. It includes intentional discipling, equipping seminars/conferences, funneling men into accountability groups and more. But I will focus on the centerpiece of our men's ministry: our Wednesday evening Band of Brothers meeting.

My experience suggests that God uses one man as the champion for every fruitful men's program. And every champion needs a team of men. So I convened a team. But I found out that the men on the team were not willing to have any "skin in the game". So I carried the weight of the ministry on my back for a few years. While God blessed the ministry during that time, it wasn't until He raised another man to join me as my two-by-two partner that the ministry really accelerated. Two men working in this way can multiply the impact tenfold, not twofold. Our gifts were different and complementary. Things that had been falling through the cracks because of lack of time or volunteer support began to get done in an excellent way.

The next critical element for us was to create a safe and fellowship-centered place for men to come. Our Band of Brothers evenings open with a time of worship and prayer. This is followed by teaching, which in turn is followed by roundtable discussion time. There was little organization of this key time element (discussion time) in the beginning. We saw that we needed to bring structure to this if men were going to get the most out of their investment of time together. So we recruited mature Christian men to become table leaders. We began communicating with them what they needed to know to be successful in this table ministry. And we continually encouraged them. In short, we came to understand that the best thing we could do for the men in Band of Brothers was focus on getting the "table leader" equipping right.

We are committed to effective training for our table leaders. Our four-hour training session is mandatory for all table leaders and prospective table leaders. It clearly lays out the role of table leaders. Every man who goes through the training has the opportunity to opt out if he is not ready to assume the complete role. The bottom line of the training is that every table leader must understand his role in discipling each man at his table.

The final element of the table leader experience is that the men's ministry leaders have consistent follow-up with the men at their tables. The communication lines are always open. We create opportunities for the table leaders to get together to talk about what's working and what's not working at their tables in a forum that protects the nonnegotiable confidentiality of the table members. This peer-to-peer time encourages and equips the table leaders to do their tasks with excellence.

The insight we gleaned after operating this way for a few years surprised our senior pastor and us: men begin attending the Band of Brothers to hear the Word of God taught, but they stay because of the authentic community that happens around the tables. Wow!

The structure we implemented to organize and build an effective men's ministry is working. We need the structure in order for our men to successfully receive all we have for them so they can be equipped as disciple makers.

Step 3: Do a Survey and Profile

Effective men's ministry programs will appeal to the interests and needs of the men of your congregation. And since the activities you undertake must be consistent with those needs, the obvious question arises: what, exactly, are the interests and needs of men in my church and community?

Let's step back for a moment to look at how Morley has categorized men, in general terms, into five types.

Type 1: Need Christ—60% of American men, your primary market!

Type 2: Cultural Christians—33% of American men, the typical churchman, "on the fringe" in the church through a sense of obligation or by (enjoyable and "busy") surface-level involvement.

Type 3: Biblical Christians—5.5% of American men, those with willing hearts, seeking a deeper faith through learning, serving, leading.

Type 4: Leaders—1% of American men, those inspired (and gifted) to help others become biblical Christians and then beyond to disciple makers, those who can influence others to join the effort.

Type 5: Hurting Men—found in each of the above categories; see chapter 10 for how to work with them.[6]

With this grid in mind, work with your team to do a congregational survey of your men. You'll use your knowledge of types of men, along with specifics about your local men, to create a smorgasbord of "entry points" that range from broad general appeal, to specific targeting of types. When you plan your events, you'll have a specific goal for the type of man you are hoping to reach.

Here's a questionnaire I've used for developing a profile. Tweak it for your own situation.

Profile of the Men of Your Congregation

1. How many men are in your congregation? You'll need to spend some time analyzing the church membership and attendance records.

2. What are the men's ministry programs in your congregation and how many men are involved in each kind of activity/event?
   a.
   b.
   c.
   d.
   e.

3. Number of full-time clergy?

4. Your congregation is (type of service): traditional, secular, contemporary, etc.

119

5. What is the average age of the men in your congregation? What is the breakdown of ages in real numbers?

6. What are the different interests of the men in your congregation (hobbies, recreational, etc.)?

7. What is the percentage of single men and married men in your congregation?
    Single:
    Married:

8. What percentage of your men are fathers of children at home?

Step 4: Create a Mission Statement

For your men's ministry to have a focus, take time to develop a dynamic vision/mission statement. This does not have to be an involved process. It will give you a chance to brainstorm with the leadership team and develop a vision to guide your ministry. Here are a few helpful hints.

1. Create your vision/mission statement with a biblically based theme.
2. Answer the following questions: What do you want to happen in your own life and in the lives of other men? How do you intend to accomplish this? How do you intend to measure your results?
3. Combine the answers into one clear, short mission statement.

For example, the First Baptist's Men's Ministry vision statement goes like this: "Encouraging men to seek the heart of God."

Mission Statement: "Providing Evangelical Zeal"

Your men's ministry vision statement:

Your men's ministry mission statement:

Remember to constantly insert your vision and mission statement in announcements, invitations and informal conversations with men wherever you are with them.

According to the top men's leaders, a ministry to men is all-inclusive in two ways. First, it includes *every man* in your church, along with the ones you *hope* will be there in the future. Second, it includes *every ministry* in your church. That is, any ministry that could help a man grow spiritually should be considered an avenue for ministry to men. With this understanding, we can take all the undifferentiated activities and see them as potential spiritual-growth avenues. It's just that *we need to be intentional about what we hope to achieve with a man's spiritual growth* and walk with him on the journey.

This is where the mission statement is crucial: if each man becomes aware that the church's goal for him is to become a committed follower of Jesus, then he will enter that activity knowing he's with a band of brothers *who will ask him how that activity is helping him grow.* They are walking with him through the learning/training experience and expecting it to take hold in his life, where it will be observable in word and deed.

Again, everything your church does that touches men is men's ministry. Thus, the size of your men's ministry is equal to the number of men in your church who are intentionally involved in growing spiritually.

Step 5: Plan Your Entry Points

It's a truism that's true: a great way to reach men is through their stomachs—pancakes, steaks and Klondike bars. Entry Points make use of these things and much more, to bring the unchurched man closer. Defined, they are guy-oriented events that invite the unchurched to meet and make friends with Christians. If you want men to hop aboard the jet of your disciple-making process, you've first got to get them onto the tarmac.

Entry points make it easy for any man to come to a church event that isn't "churchy". His first clue might be that it's likely held off the campus of your church. It might be something fun, though it might also be an entry-level ministry or service project. But whatever events you plan, they should be designed to serve as the catalyst to bring men into relationships with other men of your congregation. Consider these three categories.

1. FOOD. Though eating is a main activity here, the day or evening should include a spiritual message, video, or talk as part of the program.
   -Annual Steak Night or Pig Roast
   -Chili Cook-off
   -Monthly or quarterly men's ministry breakfasts

2. SPORTS ACTIVITIES. Consider the age-range of the group you're targeting and plan accordingly. Decide whether it would be best to make this a participatory event or a spectator event.
   -softball game
   -bowling
   -golf tournament
   -ski trip
   -hiking, etc.

-professional sports event
-watch the Super Bowl
-go to a baseball game

Sports activities are easy to organize and allow the men of your congregation to come together and build relationships in a "team spirit" context.

3. CONFERENCES AND RETREATS. Retreats are terrific ways to encourage fellowship and Christian formation. Conferences also help create momentum for a congregation's men's ministry program.

The key is that entry points are nonthreatening to the men you hope to reach. That is, they do not ask for what might make a man feel uptight, embarrassed, incompetent, or put on the spot. And to fit with your purpose of eventually making disciples, they **need these** two components: the *event itself* and the *follow-up offer*.

When a man has initiated friendship through an entry point, he is much more likely to accept an invitation to attend a *next step* that appeals to his more specific interests and needs. That's the follow-up offer—an easy step into some form of an *obviously-valuable-to-him* group, or study, or seminar. You'll craft the invitation carefully, depending on your "target audience"—the types of men you hope to reach. And you'll speak of this invitation at the beginning, middle and end of the event, where it's made obvious how to say "yes".

The *next-step* offer I refer to as **"Equipping Programs"** because they encourage spiritual growth in a particular area. For example, it might be an invitation to a six or eight-session, weekly video presentation on "how to be an authentic man" with coffee and discussion. For the unchurched entry guy, the program will be short-term, with a clearly stated end point.

In every case, make sure this man is invited to a newly formed group of similarly new men, facilitated by a mature man of your team. Don't make him suffer the awkwardness of being the "new guy" in a long-term group of men who are already tight with each other.

So, you have **entry points** at various levels, directed to particular types and profiles of men, *and* you have spiritual-formation **equipping programs.** Remember that the equipping programs are to help you close the *gap* for your men. The *gap* is the place men enter when they are inspired to follow Jesus but see their only two options as becoming an usher or going to seminary. We fill that gap by showing men the myriad forms of ministry required to carry out the mission of kingdom building and equipping them with the tools and training they need for those ministries. If we don't intentionally fill this gap in the coming decade, it will be business as usual in our mainline denominational churches with continued numerical decline, especially among men.

Since no two congregations are alike, the suggested possibilities are only a starting point. Be creative and allow God to lead you to new and more effective ways to reach the men of your congregation and community through the entry points you design. Finally, here are a few do's and don'ts.

> **DO** invite primarily through one-on-one personal invitation, which guarantees significant involvement. **DO** make sure men are also being discipled as they are enjoying activities. All events should somehow connect to your goal: to form disciple makers. The invitation to a next step is often the connection. **DO** offer prizes and trophies when you hold competitions of any kind.

DON'T forget exit points! Ask for *short-term commitments* when inviting men to the next-step equipping programs.

DON'T forget to celebrate when a man reaches the finish line, conclusion of a course, etc. A man's natural cycle is to plan, work, celebrate, rest, plan. . .

DON'T initiate too much too soon, over-schedule, or expect quick results in your ministry to men.

Step 6: Choose the Equipping Content

Here's where a key question may arise in your mind as you've come this far in our chapter: what, exactly, is the formation *content?* I offer a "pick and choose" approach that lays out the options for you in a process called AJDM: A Journey in Disciple Making.

After all, there are many programs, studies and materials out there to choose from and many are excellent. Please take the time to visit **Appendix A** for a full description of the Journey in Disciple Making content. Then it will remain for you and your men's ministry team to think through the strengths of each of the programs/studies in relation to the needs of your group and the individual growth patterns of particular men. As you explore, be sure to keep asking questions like these:

- **Will it be best for us to begin with a retreat?**
- **Would we like to initiate monthly meetings?**
- **Could we start one-to-one discipling with the goal of multiplying disciples over time?**
- **Might we gather men for a video program and meal each week for a designated period of time?**
- **What about speakers with breakfast, with table leaders and a clear next step for groupings?**

Regardless of your responses to questions like these, I know you'll find a curriculum that will allow you to develop your own equipping process for the men of your church.

Men's Bible Study, Harbor Springs Presbyterian Church, Harbor Springs, Michigan

Prayer Is the Only Way Through

I have a friend who likes to put this Latin phrase at the end of his emails: *Nil sin Deo*. It's true: "Nothing without God." You can plan your heart out and work till you drop in your ministry to men, but if your heart resides far from God, you won't harvest spiritual fruit. With God, there is no limit to what can be accomplished in the kingdom. So make prayer the engine that runs everything you do. Bathe your plans in prayer, then go back and scrub them again and again.

As you hear God leading, take your steps forward. You may need to start very small. Size the ministry to fit your church. If you're from a small church and you're asking yourself, *"How can I do all this?"* Don't be discouraged. For you, ministry to men may simply mean getting together with a different man from your church each week and asking questions. By building relationships, you are ministering to men, one at a time. As contacts are made and friendships are established, opportunities for other types of ministry will become evident.

This grassroots approach is called one-to-one discipleship, a multiplication process that starts small for big results. That's the chapter ahead.

STORY FROM THE MISSION FIELD

GEORGE WILLIAMS

I have been a Christian and an Anglican for as long as I can remember, but for the greater part of my 70-plus years, I was an insular Christian, never expressing my beliefs or sharing them with anyone or even trying to talk about my faith. My daughter, Althea, told me on several occasions that my faith is to be shared and that I should start letting people know the good things that God has done for me.

When I retired from my job as a union representative in Canada, I began spending my winters in Sarasota, Florida, where I found an Episcopal church, Church of the Redeemer. Almost immediately, I was introduced to their men's ministry. I became quite comfortable and felt accepted there. I participated in the discussions and shared my faith experiences. These meetings became the mainstay of my Christian education. I learned that men had to be encouraged to talk about their faith and share experiences that affected and impacted their lives both positively and negatively. But more importantly, they had to know that they were supported by a community of men of faith who had come to know and love God.

127

After a few years of participating at Redeemer, I decided to start up such a ministry, using the same model, at my other church in Burlington, Ontario, Canada, where I spend half the year.

Engaging in such an adventure is not an easy task and it is critical to have the backing and the total support of the rector of the parish, which I was blessed to have. The program continues to be successful and is growing. Little did I know that God could and would use me this way at age seventy-three!

Your Next-Step Action Plan

WHERE ARE YOU WITH STRUCTURE? Think back through the steps to men's ministry outlined in this chapter. Where is your church in this progression? After deciding where you are, sit down with a notebook and brainstorm your ideas about the next step to take. How would this look in your unique situation? Bring some other men in on this brainstorming and talk with your pastor about it!

For Personal Reflection

1. "Relationships are the heart and soul of ministry to men." Do I really believe this? If so, what's the state of my relationships—to Jesus Christ and to my family?

2. In what ways am I "walking the talk" these days—or not? How could I improve?

3. As I analyze my church's man-culture according to the five types of men outlined in this chapter, what do I see? If there are hurting men in my world, what is my responsibility to them?

4. Am I the one to speak to my pastor about ministry to men? What is my prayer about this?

5. I agree that prayer is the only way through. What is my prayer for the men of my community? Who will pray with me?

For Group Discussion

1. Talk about the idea of "undifferentiated priorities" in your church and among your men. How serious is the problem and what system changes might help?

2. Together, talk through each of the steps laid out in this chapter. Discuss practical ways you might begin implementing them in your particular situation.

3. Which of the steps seem the easiest to get going on? Which seem the most daunting? Why?

4. What kinds of entry points would likely work well in your church or ministry to men? Brainstorm a short list. What's the next step?

Chapter 8

Have You Heard the Call to Discipling?

Jesus believed in spiritual multiplication. He took the long view of what was necessary for a strong movement. The patient training of disciples is the only means endorsed by Scripture for building the church. . . .When churches try one crash program after another without strengthening the body of disciples, volumes of time and energy are wasted. If our ministries do not lead to the making of obedient fruit-bearing believers, then we have simply "fattened up" the church.

Bill Hull[1]

The little town of Moultrie, Georgia, sits in the southwest corner of the state, about 40 miles above the Florida state line. It is a town that time has mostly forgotten. Once it was a training center for pilots during World War II. Now it boasts a large chicken-processing plant, but still remains in its own world, surrounded by cotton fields, peanut farms and groves of pecan trees. The Christians there are mostly Baptists of one stripe or another. There is no Lutheran or Mennonite church, for example and no synagogue.

However, some Christian pastors in a few of the churches there decided upon a rather radical concept: suppose we thought of "church growth" as an adventure in producing *depth* rather than just width? And suppose this were actually the biblical way of doing things, the way of Jesus Himself?

I'll pick up the Moultrie story again at the end of the chapter, showing you how these pastors reached men in a marvelous process of multiplication. For now, though, let's think about the "depth charge" concept and why it matters to every church leader.

Disciple Making: It's Not an Option Anymore!

If the American church faces a crisis, it's not merely a numbers problem. It's a Christian maturity crisis and that more foundational problem, I believe, can be overcome only by welcoming back the men. But welcoming them back to what? To a deeper relationship with God the Father and His Son, Jesus. That is the "depth charge", the mandate that comes directly from our Lord and His apostles: make disciples (Matthew 28:19) and multiply the disciple makers (2 Timothy 2:2).

Dear church leader, if I can convince you of the centrality of this mandate, your approach to ministry will be turned upside down.

In 2011, the C. S. Lewis Institute launched a new initiative to get churches excited and involved in the church-renewing potential of a discipleship focus. Here are some of the reasons cited for their renewed emphasis, stressing that "even growing churches are having problems."

- Only half of Christians believe in absolute moral truth. (Barna)

- Numerous studies show that self-identified Christians are living lives indistinguishable from non-Christians. (Jim Houston)
- Of self-identified Christians, 27% believe Jesus sinned while on earth. (Barna)
- Atheists, agnostics and Mormons scored better on biblical literacy than evangelical Christians. (Pew Research)
- Of those who have walked away from the church, 65% report having given their lives to Christ at some point in their youth. (Barna)
- Growing churches typically have large youth programs, but only 3% of young people professing faith in Christ are living lives of solid faith. (Barna)
- Almost 9 out of 10 senior pastors of Protestant churches asserted that spiritual immaturity is one of the most serious issues facing the church. (Barna)[2]

The report went on to say that Willow Creek, a growing "mega church" near Chicago, produced three studies of its congregation and hundreds of other churches. From their research they are shifting their focus from a "seeker-friendly" approach to a more balanced path of helping people reach spiritual maturity. Dr. John Stott, the late beloved Anglican pastor and author, sums it up: "We acknowledge that the state of the church is marked by a paradox of growth without depth. Our zeal to go wider has not been matched by a commitment to go deeper."[3]

This is not a dry, academic problem for sociological research. We are talking about real people here amidst deep pain. We need to reach them and mentor them into the deeper life for transformed hearts. Consider these statistics from the National Coalition of Men's Ministries. Though these numbers come from the 1990s, realize that this means things have likely gotten worse:[4]

- One in 22 men will suffer from depression.
- One in 11 men will go to prison.
- One in 4 men will cheat on his wife (versus 1-in-8 wives).
- More men are their children's primary, live-in caretakers, from 393,000 in 1970 to 1.3 million in 1994.
- More than 24 million children (36%) live without their biological father.
- There are 1.9 million single fathers with children under 18.

Making disciples is a means of extending warm and direct compassion to men like these, putting faces and hearts to the statistics. It's a holistic healing: a disciple is a man who is following Christ (head), being changed by Christ (heart) and becoming committed to his mission (hands). He is one who purposes each day to live above sin. But here's the key: He has a mentor to lead him into all of this. Evangelical men's writer Gordon Dalbey tells us that men yearn for this kind of one-to-one relationship after the era of Promise Keepers: "We've been to two or three stadium events, but we need much more. Take us deeper."[5]

The goal is no longer just to bring the lost into the fold—which is crucial, of course—but *to make mature spiritual reproducers*. The dynamic thing is that the process of discipling men uses every situation in life's laboratory as a classroom to teach, to plant seeds, to nurture those seeds and to await the blossoming of a new missionary—the equipped man.

The statistics above may provide enough rationale for putting disciple making at the heart of a church's mission, but consider two more stellar reasons for committing to a disciple-making welcome for men in your church and community: (1) the attractiveness of Jesus and (2) the biblical call—and our need—for spiritual fathering.

We must offer the attractiveness of Jesus. He is our model. We must be discipled by the Master Himself to make disciples that look like Him and reproduce like Him.

Why Jesus? Because "without Him, we can do nothing" (John 15:5); because we are His body on earth — the only true God the world can see; because He's the most compelling Man for men in pursuing the abundant life. As the apostle Paul put it,

> *He is the one we proclaim,* admonishing and teaching everyone with all wisdom, *so that we may present everyone fully mature in Christ. To this end I strenuously contend with all the energy Christ so powerfully works in me.* (Colossians 1:28, 29)

Paul's words echo what poured from the lips of Jesus Himself when He gave the Great Commission in Matthew 28. His final command was to make disciples, long before there was an established, organized church. He said, in effect: "You see Me? This is how I want you to be, too. And the image of Myself, reflected in you, is to be reproduced in others through your mentoring influence." C. S. Lewis once spoke of this as the ultimate purpose for our salvation, that every one of us become a "little Christ".

If we agree with this statement, how shall we go about helping men fully achieve this, their truest identity? One take on this is the perspective of Bill Hull in his book *Jesus Christ, Disciplemaker.* Hull ties the New Testament's discipling commands to the 1ˢᵗ century rabbinical education process. "Every Jewish boy by age thirteen had studied and memorized much of the Pentateuch and the prophets. If he was among the best and the brightest, he would be accepted into a rabbinical school. There he would come under the authority of his teacher." Hull points to five characteristics of these ancient "schools".[6]

134

1. The disciple chose to submit to his teacher.
2. The disciple would memorize his teacher's words.
3. The disciple would learn his teacher's way of ministry.
4. The disciple would imitate his teacher's life.
5. The disciple would be expected to find his own disciples.

Now Jesus was a rabbi and He took up such practices as His primary approach to winning the world for the kingdom of heaven. It would start so small, like a mustard seed and become the biggest tree of all. Consider what this meant.

First, Jesus looked for those whose hearts were willing to submit to Him and His mission. Second, He would pour His words into a few select men so they could memorize them and make them central to their core *being*. Third, by a process of apprenticeship training—filled with trial and error!—He would teach His way of *doing* ministry among people. Fourth, He would be with them, constantly modeling His ways before them, so that His very life would be "caught" by them in a virtually unconscious imitation. Fifth, He would not be satisfied until these disciples became disciple makers themselves, *reproducing* what He had built into them.

Being, training by doing, reproducing. Could we really improve on the methods of Jesus?

Over the years, it has been stated, "We have found too many ways to be Christians without being Christ-like." When we begin to see Christ as He is, however, we're attracted to a better way. No longer do we attempt to entice men into the church based only on the "program" we offer them. Rather, we set before them our Savior, who said, "And I, if I am lifted up from the earth, will draw all peoples to Myself" (John 12:32).

In other words, let the program lead them to the Person.

There is one caveat here: in some quarters, to be like Jesus is to be a real man's man, an ultra-masculine tough guy who rides motorcycles and plays sandlot, tackle football with the guys. We walk on dangerous ground with such an idea. Discipleship is for both men and women, of course. We are all called to emulate Him. Every type of man, from the sensitive guy who loves poetry to the Seal Team Six warrior, can take on the character of Christ.

The point is the gifts of the Spirit are neither masculine nor feminine. Nor did Jesus come to show us what masculinity is. Therefore, if we find traits in women that distinguish them from men generally, we'll expect their growth in Christ to perfect those traits. The clearest picture of Jesus will come through to us only when we take the most objective reading of the Gospels as we can.

We must promote spiritual fathering. Welcoming men back with a desire to love them to Jesus is a form of spiritual fathering. It's a term that tells us *every man should be producing spiritual sons.* Any man who hopes to become such a father will be the warmest and most hospitable person. In effect, he will be emulating the father of the wandering son in Luke 15. This is the father who "saw him and had compassion, and ran and fell on his neck and kissed him" (Luke 15:20).

It is fairly common to hear in men's ministry circles that every man needs other men to play at least three crucial roles in his life. He needs a Paul (a mentor), a Barnabas (an encourager) and a Timothy (a disciple). Someone will be his spiritual father, someone will constantly encourage his growth in discipleship and he will, in turn, take on a "son" to mentor into a reproducer of other disciples.

This is essential because the spiritual life is more like a long-distance race than a sprint. This means that even more than pumping knowledge into a new believer, we need to develop and maintain a strong relationship with him over the years. As I look into the pages of the Bible, I see the parenting approach everywhere. Paul took Timothy as his son in the Lord. Peter spoke of obedient children. The apostle John called his readers "little children". And Christ once spoke of Himself as a hen with her chicks. Even the book of Hebrews tells of a spiritual infancy and maturity, in which the younger needed to become grown-ups.

It's true that as you begin to see yourself as a potential father to a less mature Christian, you'll need wise discernment in determining his "level" of Christian maturity. Stages are in play here. Men are believers, but they may be babies, children, adolescents, or young adults in the faith. Or they may be ready to become spiritual parents themselves.

So find someone from whom you can learn and someone else whom you can take to the next level in their walk with the Lord. "The role of the spiritual parent is to keep new Christians close to the Spirit," writes Phil Downer, president of Discipleship Network of America. "Let them see how God has changed your life. Reveal your God-given perspective and values to them, so they can begin to think in a whole new way. Remember, our goal is not to change all of the world at once, but to help change one life at a time. As God works through us as spiritual parents, we'll see him change other people from the inside out."[7]

This is not just about imparting knowledge or getting someone into the Scriptures, as important as knowledge is. Rather, you hope to move a man through a process, in this relationship, to the point that he is trained to *do ministry.*

But How Do I Disciple This Man?

I read somewhere that a medical school student, training to be a surgeon, was told, "See one, do one, teach one." Watch a surgery, do the surgery (under the watchful eyes of a master), then teach it to others—many times over. The principle holds in discipling: we take a man with us to watch how we lead a class or work with an individual or minister in an outreach setting. We invite him to try it himself, time and again, as we watch and debrief. Then we eventually release him to take another with him to watch him do ministry.

This training process normally takes at least a year and the feedback process is ongoing for a lifetime. We are always available to that disciple, even though we've now taken others under our wing.

Let's say that you look around your church and you see "nothing much happening" for the men. Let's suppose, too, you are in a smaller church with a limited budget and personnel resources. Let's further suppose that your heart has been moved to disciple-making, whether you are a pastor or a layman.

The key for you is *not* to try to implement big programs right off the bat. Pour over the first part of this chapter and the rationale it presents for disciple-making. Then begin to consider what it would mean for you to fit the ministry to the church.

The response that comes to my mind is simply this: start small. Start with just one man. And why not? Jesus spread His ministry one man at a time.

Could you ask a different man to meet with you each week and just ask some questions? Could you ask one man out to lunch and at some point ask, "How are you doing?" Listen. Then ask, "No, really. . . how are you doing?" You will be amazed at how effective this simple approach will be. But, your interest must be sincere.

Pray, pray, pray. God will lead you in this. It is His work, after all and He certainly cares for the souls of men—even more than we do. Just keep the words from the book of 2 Timothy constantly in mind:

> *The things that you have heard from me among many witnesses, commit these to faithful men who will be able to teach others also.* (2 Timothy 2:2)

138

These are your marching orders: Go make disciple makers.

The Rest of the Story: A Little Town that Could!

Now, I promised to tell you the rest of the story of Moultrie, Georgia. That was the little town where some pastors of various churches got together to take men's discipleship seriously. All of this was conveyed to me by one of those pastors, who "wrote it up" in the local newspaper, *The Moultrie Observer.* So I'll let him tell it in his own words, for your inspiration.

> **Can there really be such a thing as an anonymous Christian? I do know that we are the body of Christ, and the members of this body must work together closely for optimum healthy functioning. Even in the huge church, members gather and find close fellowship in smaller groups and classes. And this is as it should be, for there is something about community that is absolutely essential. We need the fellowship, the support, and the prayers that mutual caring brings.**
>
> **In fact, the biblical vision has little to do with being a "lone ranger" follower. The Lord calls us to grow in righteousness and love, but we can't do it alone. We need to help one another in this process. In fact, we have that blessed responsibility—and will very likely be held accountable someday for our efforts.**
>
> **Now let me tell you about something that is happening right here in Moultrie along these lines. It's called personal discipleship. Here's how it works: a man or woman who has matured (to some degree) in the Christian faith takes another**

person under their wing to help them grow in spiritual maturity, as well. It involves meeting with that "disciple" regularly, usually for an hour a week.

What happens in those meetings? Quite simply, the two seek to become more committed disciples of Jesus. They typically choose a portion of Scripture to read together, and then ask the question: "What does this mean—and what does it mean to you, right now?"

Further, the discipler will ask: "How do you hope to apply this in your life?" The two will talk about very practical and specific applications of biblical principles that come through. Then there may be a time of prayer for one another.

Each week there will be follow-up—"How is it going?"—with the specific efforts of each disciple. Underlying it all, though, is simply learning to surrender to God's presence and leading, each moment of every day. And experiencing the joy of the Lord in return.

The result of such efforts at obeying Christ's command to "make disciples" has been phenomenal in our town. David Brown, of Good Samaritan Counseling, spearheaded the effort a year ago, starting with just a handful of men, myself included. He now reports about 130 men, from various churches, large and small, involved in this kind of discipleship (with some 30 women, as well). Most of these pairs meet at Good Samaritan's offices or at St. John's Episcopal Church, while others meet at various workplaces and offices.

The movement grows by multiplication, 2 Timothy 2:2—"The things you have heard me say in the presence of many witnesses entrust to reliable men who will also be qualified to teach others." This multiplication of disciples is exactly how the body of Christ is called to grow. That's why each disciple is asked to seek God's leading in finding someone that they, too, can take under their wing in this blessed mentoring process.

It is the antithesis of the anonymous, lone-ranger mentality, and it is clearly blessed by God.[8]

In our next chapter, let's get practical about the "how to" of this discipling process. We'll look more closely at the nuts and bolts by considering four aspects of this process: selecting your disciple, modeling and pouring your life, establishing accountability and avoiding the discipling pitfalls.

Your Next-Step Action Plan

JOURNAL IT! Look again at the statistics from the National Coalition of Men's Ministries about men's depression, prison, fatherless children and so on. Begin journaling your thoughts as you check the daily news stories online or in your local newspaper—stories that have any relation to these stats. Make the men in your culture a matter of serious prayer and ask God to open your eyes to the plight of men in your own neighborhood, workplace and world.

For Personal Reflection

1. Do I agree that disciple making is not optional? So what does this mean for me, personally?

2. As I study the statistics given in this chapter, what are my conclusions related to this chapter's emphasis on depth?

3. The methods of Jesus were simple, yet powerful and effective: being, training by doing, reproducing. Why would the church feel it could improve on these methods? What about my men's ministry?

4. Who are, or have been, spiritual fathers to me? In what ways? Who am I fathering these days?

For Group Discussion

1. What is your understanding of the term *spiritual multiplication*? How willing are you to take up this approach?

2. "If the American church faces a crisis, it's not merely a numbers problem. It's a Christian maturity crisis." Talk about this while referring to the "depth charge" idea.

3. In light of 2 Timothy 2:2, discuss the difference between a disciple and a disciple maker. What is the process of moving from one to the other?

4. What would it mean for your men's ministry, in the most practical terms, to offer the attractiveness of Jesus? Refer to the Lord's rabbinic methods.

5. Talk together about your experiences of "spiritual fathering". Are you a "spiritual son" and/or do you *have* one (or more)?

Chapter 9

Do You Know the Nuts and Bolts of Disciple Making?

It all started when I first came to the Lord as a senior in high school. John, the college student who led me to the Lord, spent six months meeting with me on a weekly basis, if not more, to instruct me and build into me the basics of being a disciple of Jesus. Through Bible study, long walks together, serving together, and learning to share my faith, he helped me see that to be a follower of Jesus was an adventure. . . and I had the responsibility to do for others what he did for me.

Steve Sonderman[1]

Most men, especially when they get a little older, think about the legacy they'll leave behind. Disciple making has a lot to do with our legacy. Think of what you'd like to be known for once you've left this earth. Is it the amount of projects you completed in your work? Or maybe the accumulation of "toys" you've stashed in your garage? Barbara Bush once put it in perspective when she said, "No one ever came to the end of their life thinking, 'I wish I'd spent more time at the office.'"

No, we'd rather think we spent good, quality time with our family and friends and that we accomplished something of lasting significance. When it comes to leaving a legacy as an authentic Christian man, consider this noble possibility: you are remembered as a man who discipled a few other men, who discipled others, who discipled still others. You will be remembered as a spiritual grandfather.

Billy Graham won thousands to Christ during his crusades. But I'm thinking right now of another person whose legacy may be even greater: the man who won Billy Graham to Christ. Do you know his name? More important, does God know his name? I'm thinking even the angels and demons know his name—Mordecai Ham.

It's like that with discipling. One man on earth can quietly create a multitude in heaven. Now, are you ready to see what it takes to begin the discipleship approach to multiplying a legacy?

Identifying and Inviting a Potential Timothy

If you are a Christian man, maturing in the faith and inspired by the Great Commission, you'll eventually desire a "Timothy" to mentor. He'll be your spiritual son, who someday will give you spiritual grandsons (see 2 Timothy 2:1; Philemon 1:10). But how do you find him? Take three steps.

1. *Consider the "ideal" disciple and start the search there.* Ideally, he will be someone you like, who is available, who is interested and who is teachable. Pat Morley says, "The greatest return on your time will come from investing in a few 'FATS' men—men who are *faithful, available, teachable, stable.*"[2]

I like the F.A.T.S. idea and here's what it means in practical terms. A *faithful* guy is one in whom you've observed this: he does what he says. The *available* guy isn't too busy. This is a tough hurdle. Many, many guys are just too busy. They really aren't ready, just from a time perspective, to take on even an hour a week of personalized training. You'll have to bypass the busy guy for now (though keep encouraging him at any level he can receive). The *teachable* guy is saying in no uncertain terms, "I really want to learn and grow." And you find that he follows through on what you ask him to do. The *stable* guy has the basic self-discipline and self-control established in his character so that he won't suddenly flip out on you with no warning.

Your potential Timothy certainly will have to be willing to be accountable. The encouraging thing to remember is that he will have been prepared in advance by the Holy Spirit with a desire to grow in Christ.

In mainline churches, the common trait of a potential disciple is that he's been a Christian for years, but *not* a reproducer. He's a "Decade Man"—a church member for at least a decade, maybe serving as an usher all those years. My denomination, the Episcopal Church, is swarming with these guys, along with the "cradle Episcopalians". They're good guys, certainly spiritual to some degree—perhaps even committed to attending a daily mass. They are spiritual, but not spiritually mature. The decade man may even be living a secret life to some degree. As someone has said, "He was going to heaven, but making hellacious decisions along the way." But God can transform even the decade man.

Perhaps it goes without saying that your first disciple-ship responsibility is with your own family. That is your "Jerusalem" in Acts 1:8. Don't think about branching out from there until you're sure you and your own household are growing in Christian maturity.

> **2. Pray. . . then pray some more.** Who are the men you could imagine being "on fire" for the Lord some day? Who needs some help and is willing to receive it? Pray!

Start to think in terms of "divine appointments" here. Begin to expect that as you pray and as you interact with all kinds of men in your world, a man is going to stand out to you at some point as "ripe for the picking". Surely God must prepare him for you with an open heart and if that is so, then God is not going to hide him from you. Sensitize your own spirit to the leading of God's Spirit. Keep your eyes open for that willing man.

Jesus spent all night in prayer before calling the original disciples to follow Him. We'll want to make it a constant prayer for guidance, too. The key is our heart of love for the men God brings into our paths daily.

It can help to begin making a list of men you will be praying for. Then trust God; He is the one who will choose.

3. *Go ahead; ask him.* When you have a pretty clear sense of who your Timothy could be, go ahead and invite him. There are at least two effective approaches here. One is to invite him to a no-commitment pre-meeting. It's purely exploratory. You'll lay out the purpose, process and goals. Be clear about the stringency of the requirements for attendance. You require a weekly meeting, at least one hour, for at least six months. Let your potential disciple think it over and get back to you. If he doesn't get back to you. . . well, you have your answer, right?

I call this way the Reach 3 method. In my church, disciple makers commit to writing three names on a card—men they'll invite to lunch, individually, at some point during the coming year. I am now going to reemphasize one of the most important discipling tools from the previous chapter. After some easy small talk we will look into that potential disciple's eyes and ask with all seriousness, "How are you doing?" When the man has responded with the typical "Just fine, no problems, great," we then ask again, "No, really. . . how are you doing?" Then we sit back and listen. The ensuing conversation often results in developing a discipling relationship.

TAKE THE REACH 3 CHALLENGE!*

Prayerfully identify **three men** you know who are not Christians from your work, neighborhood, and/or recreation.

1. _____
2. _____
3. _____

- Pray for these men every day—for their salvation, families, jobs, etc.
- Invite each man to a one-on-one meal, with no agenda, to just get to know them.
- Consider asking for specific prayer requests as it seems appropriate. Remember to ask, "How are you doing. . . *really?*"
- As you get to know them over weeks and months, invite them to an outreach event and/or entry point at your church.
- they decide to make a commitment to Christ, help them become involved in church and discipleship opportunities.

*Carry these in your wallet! Attractive cards, business size, with this info on it, are available from Jay Crouse, Men and the Church, 941.320.0271, jaycrouse@aol.com.

A second approach is to use a card that you hand to men to test their FATness before doing anything else. For example, one pastor[3] uses a business card with Philippians 3:10 printed on one side: "I want to know Christ and the power of his resurrection and the fellowship of sharing in his sufferings, becoming like him in his death."

When he comes across a guy who might be a potential Timothy, he hands this man the card and says something along these lines: "I've been praying for men over the last few months and I'm looking for men who might be sensing a need for deeper growth in the faith. *Would you take this card and memorize the verse on the front?* There are some other verses printed on the other side, too. But get back with me when you've got the Philippians verse memorized." He keeps a running record of who he's given out the cards to.

He eventually checks back and asks the man whether he has memorized the verse yet. If the guy responds in the affirmative, his next question is: "What did it mean to you?" Now the door is wide open for a potential invitation to one-on-one discipleship meetings. If the answer is no, the pastor says something like: "Well, if you are still interested, would you keep trying and get back to me?" He won't bring it up again unless the individual comes to him first.[4]

The point is that rather than trying to find disciples through making an announcement in the church bulletin or putting up posters around town, just quietly approach a man, here and there, as God leads you.

Modeling and Pouring the Christian life

Someone has said that men today aren't looking for *answers*, but for *examples*. Jesus was an example, intentionally and intensively, to 12 men. Since He worked with them individually and as a group, you'll want to do the same. Eventually, get your men into groups, too.

Then show them how to lead a group by a process of apprenticeship. For example, if you set up a group and you facilitate it, always have a man in training who will eventually take over leadership. Be looking for one or two in the group who could be apprentices, so you can move to setting up another group from your one-to-one disciple meetings. When you have five guys, gather them in a group, then develop an apprentice from that group. Those apprentices will also be doing exactly the same multiplication of their efforts with others, who in turn will do the same and on and on and on. They've observed you doing it and you've intentionally shown them how.

It's ultimately a life-to-life relationship of modeling the truth and ministry of the gospel and pouring your own life into another. You are saying to a man, "I am going to *be* the love of the Father to you!" The apostle Paul put it like this: "Imitate me, just as I also imitate Christ" (1 Corinthians 11:1).

Now, what do you actually do in your one-to-one sessions? The answers vary among those who disciple, but the basic purpose is always the same: I'm imparting what I know and the skills I have to someone else who will eventually do the same with another man.

Quite simply, the two men encourage one another to become more deeply committed disciples of Jesus. As I mentioned in the previous chapter, the men will usually choose a Bible passage to read together and then discuss how it applies to them in their real-life situations. They'll also go through some accountability questions before praying with and for one another.

Game Plan for Gathering

> *"And they continued steadfastly in the apostles' doctrine and fellowship, in the breaking of bread, and in prayers."*(Acts 2:42)

START OFF
- How has God blessed you this week? What went right in your life?

- What problem consumed your thoughts this week? What went wrong?

SPIRITUAL LIFE

- Have you read God's Word during the week? Talk about it.
- Describe your prayers concerning yourself, others, praise, confession.
- How is your relationship with Christ?
- Have you been tempted this week? How did you respond?
- Do you have any unconfessed sin?
- Are you walking in the Spirit?
- Did you worship in church this week? Talk about that.
- Have you shared your faith? In what ways?

HOME LIFE

- How is it going with your wife/girlfriend/significant other: attitudes, time, irritations disappointments, her faith?
- How is it going with your children: quality and quantity of time, education, spiritual welfare, values, and beliefs?
- How are your finances: debts, sharing, stewardship, saving?

WORK LIFE

- How are things going with your commitments: job, volunteer, projects, career progress, relationships, workload, stress, temptations?

CRITICAL CONCERNS

- Do you feel in the center of God's will? Do you sense His peace?

- What are you wrestling with in your thought life these days?
- What have you done for someone else this week?
- Are your priorities in the right order?
- Is your moral and ethical behavior what it should be?
- How are you doing in your personal high-risk areas of temptation or addiction?
- Is the "visible" you and the "real" you consistent in this relationship?

Final Question: Have you lied to me about anything?

Adapted from
Man in the Mirror **by Pat Morley**

Realize that a quick Google search of "accountability questions for men" will give you plenty of ideas about standard questions to raise with each other every time you meet. Fit them to your particular personalities.

But do you need a more specific plan or curriculum to follow for the one-to-one sessions? There are myriad good books and programs available! Here are four of my favorites.

- *One2Won Crosstraining, by Joe White.* Available from menathecross.org. This is my absolute favorite, since it takes a man through 24 individual sessions and begins, at week 12, to help him think and train for becoming his own disciple maker. Its focus is on "loving a man to Jesus until he's ready to love another man to Jesus."
- *Seeking Him: Experiencing the Joy of Personal Revival, by Tim Grissom and Nancy Leigh DeMoss.*

Available from Life Action Revival Ministries: http://seekinghim.com/community

This is a 12-week experience in personal, spiritual revival. The study was inspired by Psalm 69:32b: "You who seek God, let your hearts revive." Each interactive lesson features five days of individual study followed by a group discussion section. Participants are renewed and revitalized as they explore honesty, humility, repentance, grace, obedience and other topics. This is an ideal small-group program; however, two men could commit to going through it together, meeting weekly to compare notes.

- *Daily Study Bible for Men,* with daily studies by Stuart Briscoe. Available from Tyndale House Publishers: 800-323-9400. Hey, why not just use the Bible? But with this edition, you and your Timothy can choose which men's topical studies to focus on during the year of your meeting together.
- *Manual:* **The Bible for Men.** Available from Zondervan Publishers: 1-800-CHRISTIAN. Here's a snippet of the description from www.amazon.com:

Motivates men to redeem their God-given passions, drives and purposes so they can live out their faith. Features:
- 100 "Myth" articles—A common, accepted myth from the world is followed by the first-person story of a man who struggled with the lie and how it affected his life. . .
- 50 factoid profiles about select men of the Bible. . .
- 200 "Downshift" notes—Penetrating questions for personal reflection or small-group study. . .

- 300 "At Issue" notes—Short teaching notes on life topics such as money, sex, or pride, that are linked topically.

In everything you do, keep before you the foundational goals of your discipling efforts. David R. Hopkins, in *Multiplying Disciples,* states them like this:[5]

1. **Identify the preparation of each candidate for discipleship. In other words, evaluate the spiritual depth through questioning and insight from the Holy Spirit. Is he an [involved] church member? How do actions compare with words?**
2. **Assist the person in his or her personal move from a passive, non-committal position as a Christian to becoming an active follower of Jesus Christ determined to lead others to Him.**
3. **Assist each disciple in the one-to-one format to take stock of his position in Christ and to take responsibility for continual spiritual growth throughout life.**
4. **Help each person learn to hear and to obey the voice of God through the Word and the Holy Spirit.**
5. **Convince each person discipled to become a disciple maker through one-to-one witnessing and teaching.**

Avoid These Discipling Pitfalls!

Part of the discipling process is being ready to do problem solving when issues arise. What are some of those issues that we could consider pitfalls?

- **Expecting someone to be just like me.** The point is, we're all different. Christ's work is not to suppress a personality or to change it into another personality. It is to infuse that unique person with His Spirit in all areas of his life. All Scripture is "God's Word", yet each book of the Bible has the imprint of each author's unique personality, approach to literature, vocabulary, life experience, dreams, desires and goals. Likewise, God is able to take all that is in our lives and make us whole men, unique in our own personalities, mirroring the surpassing qualities of the indwelling Christ.

- **Failing to make expectations clear up front.** The bottom line, in the most candid language I can bring to bear, is this: "You *can't* meet with me unless you commit unequivocally." However, there are two important factors to keep in mind here: (1) Don't assume an "open-ended" mentoring period. Instead, at the beginning of the relationship, determine an "end date" that can be renegotiated, if desired. (2) Beware of putting *undue expectations* on a man. Be reasonable. Use discernment in each case. For example, know what "God language" a man brings to the relationship (see chapter 11) and be careful about this particular man's abilities and desires with regard to a reading program or other requirements. Gear the mentoring to the man.

- **Falling into a purely performance-based relationship.** Phil Downer, president of Discipleship Network of America (DNA), says, "One of the most common pitfalls of parenting is a performance-based relationship. We often make the same mistake in parenting our disciples that we make in our families: making our children, both spiritual and natural, feel that our love and acceptance depends on their performance. Performance-based discipleship can lead to legalism and is always destructive. Remember the disciple isn't living to please you; he's living to please God."[6]

- **Over controlling and overprotecting.** Disciples are primarily *learners*. So let them learn! And since mistakes and failures are such great teachers, let them try, experiment and fail. Jesus did this all the time. Remember when the disciples came back to Jesus, totally discouraged with their efforts at casting out demons? They had tried and failed and were ready to receive more training.

- **Conducting non-reproductive discipleship that stays in house.** George Barna says this can happen: "People in small groups are satisfied by the *process* without regard for the *progress*."[7]

  This is the case of ingrown discipling that's akin to navel gazing. Our goal is to bring people to Christ and then help them live as "Christ-ones". So the reaching out part has got to remain a priority.

- **Refusing to let him go.** We need to know when a disciple is ready to take on a disciple for himself. Then we must let him do it, as we stay available for coaching. The criteria for this readiness are pretty clear-cut. He is ready when: (1) he easily accepts direction and correction; (2) he is inspired to help other men and has demonstrated his willingness and ability to do so, as he has been observed by you in real life; (3) he has a good grasp on Scripture and biblical theology as a "grid" through which he can answer another's questions; (4) he is other-oriented with his time and energies; and (5) he is walking by the Spirit and evidences the Spirit's fruits in daily life (see Galatians 5:22, 23).

We've considered the nuts and bolts of personal mentoring and we've looked at the pitfalls to avoid in the relationship. But what about the men out there who are hurting? They'll need a skilled men's leader to help lead them on the pathways to healing. That is a specific kind of "readiness to welcome" as we seek a bright future for men in the church. Our next chapter will delve into a few heartfelt hurts that are common among men.

STORY FROM THE MISSION FIELD

FRANK FRYE

As a new believer of two years, I was discipled by a group in the Navy, the Navigators. I had been taught to pray and ask God for a man I could invest in spiritually. So at the age of 22, in an effort to answer this call (Matthew 28:18, 19) and having the desire to be a faithful disciple of Christ, I began to pray for God to show me a man (open the door to a relationship) to focus on.

God is and was faithful. His name was Bill, a junior in high school. He was eager to know more about God and had come to Christ two years earlier. My wife and I were teaching a high school Sunday school class with several of Bill's friends. I invited them all out to breakfast and presented a challenge to seek God more deeply. Four of them wanted to pursue God.

As we did a weekly Bible study, I also met with Bill individually to answer many of his questions and get to know him. He wrote his testimony and practiced how to engage people with his spiritual journey. I began to take him with me as I went on the naval base to share the gospel with sailors. We invited them to a Friday night "gathering" (singing, sharing) and Bible study.

As Bill grew in the study of the Scriptures, he followed me to service projects (roofing houses, car care for single women in the ministry, etc.) as we learned together the value of being servants for Christ. When Bill started junior college, we met for lunch on campus to share Christ with his fellow students. He continued to grow in his faith as he saw God work in the lives of those he encountered. The encouragement of others, as they grew together, was an integral part of his discipleship process.

Bill submitted each area of his life to the lordship of Christ to be available and usable for God. As he continued to pursue his degree, he gave God first priority in all of his life decisions and blossomed even more spiritually as he experienced God's guidance in his life. Throughout Bill's college years, I would meet to pray with him, encourage him and be involved in his life. Through his time in Scripture, Bill saw and understood the vision for discipleship in the lives of others and became committed to 2 Timothy 2:2 as a lifestyle. His secular vocation took him to Asia for several years, where he was able to minister in another culture and see God raise up foreign national disciples.

Today Bill is the director of missions for a global mission organization. Leading and imparting Jesus's vision for evangelism and discipleship is his passion. His journey confirms the process Jesus prayed for in John 17:20-23. As we are obedient in discipleship, Jesus's legacy in the lives of people is carried to the next generation.

Our job in discipleship, then, is to love God's man, take him to the Scriptures, pray for, encourage, challenge and stretch him and impart vision to him. Begin to pray excitedly, expectantly for God to introduce you to His man in whom you are to invest.

Your Next-Step Action Plan

WITH DISCIPLING — JUST START! When it comes to finding a Timothy to mentor, we must "pray, then pray some more." Begin making a list of potential Timothys you could mentor in the faith. Then determine to spend several weeks just praying over those names, lifting those men before the Lord. Ask God to show you whom to approach for the possibility of starting a discipling relationship. Be sure to take into account the F.A.T.S. principle.

For Personal Reflection

1. When I come to the end of my life, what kind of legacy do I hope to leave behind?

2. Who, in my world these days, is a potential Timothy? Or do I need to be spiritually fathered first before I find my own Timothy?

3. Who, specifically, are some men I could imagine "being on fire for the Lord" some day?

4. Men today aren't looking for *answers* but for *examples*. What kind of example am I looking for? What kind of example am I to other men?

For Group Discussion

1. Have you ever *been* a Timothy, formally or informally? Have you ever *had* a Timothy? Talk about it.

2. How can "one man on earth quietly create a multitude in heaven"?

3. How would you compare and contrast the process of discipling a Timothy to mentoring in the business world?

4. Discuss the statement that every man's "Jerusalem" must be his family first (see Acts 1:8).

5. Talk about the Reach 3 method and how it might work in your church and men's ministry.

Chapter 10

Can You Pastor Their Hearts?

Now that we are ten years old, we realize that for men's ministry to truly be maximized...the masculine context has got to be understood on the local church level, and pastors have got to connect with men.
Bill McCartney, Promise Keepers founder[1]

Here's the story, as my friend Gary tells it.

When I was only ten, my cancer-ridden young father took me with him to the hospital to get his next cobalt radiation treatment. Once inside that antiseptic room, standing next to a huge machine that would shoot cell-killing rays into Dad's swollen abdomen, I watched as he slowly undressed. I didn't know what to do. I needed explanations, warmth, assurance—at the very least some acknowledgment of my bewilderment: "Gary, you are afraid, sad, angry, and rightfully so, for your dad is leaving soon. And that will be tough."

Instead, the male nurse in charge put on a jovial act, cajoling me into being cheerful with him. If only I could have seen in the face of my father, not just the physical pain he was in, but the pain of my own life at that point, mirrored in his eyes.

Though it's been more than four decades since he died, I still want to know the man whose picture sits on my shelf.[2]

Five Secret Cries in Men's Hearts

R emember Chapter 4 and our look at what's in men's minds? Now let's move down from the head and see the flipside of those assumptions: the wounds of the heart. The first "heart cry" of hurting men speaks directly to Gary. . . and to most of us.

HEART CRY #1: "Heal my father wound!"

If we could enter the hearts of countless men and listen closely, we'd hear the echo of this mournful cry from the lips of the biblical Esau: "Bless me—me too, my father!" No matter how old we are, we still seek the blessing and loving approval of our parents. For a man, that means a heart yearning to hear his father convey, with voice and eyes: "Son, I'm so proud of you. May all you are and do be blessed." Even Jesus, the incarnate Son of the heavenly Father, apparently needed to hear words of blessing before starting on his earthly mission.

> *And suddenly a voice came from heaven, saying, "This is My beloved Son, in whom I am well pleased."* (Matthew 3:17)

I'm sure those words empowered Jesus, energized Him and must have helped Him through tough periods of trepidation and anxiety. A man is blessed if he's had that kind of blessing from Dad. But many men have never heard such things; they've been abandoned by their fathers in one way or another, either physically or emotionally.

This abandonment is known as the "father wound" and I have yet to find a man who can't relate to it, at one level or another. Can you, leader of men, pastor that man?

The boy in so many of us men still cries out. And that cry takes various forms in any man who has experienced the trauma of paternal abandonment, each plea reflecting the pain of a foundational loss: *"Dad, please don't leave me!"*

Even when we look at Jesus, the man, we find a time in His life when He felt abandoned by the Father. At the cross we hear three clear cries ringing out as He faced His own aloneness.

> **Abba!** Yes, the Father was really His "Daddy". . .
> **Why have you left me?** Yes, Jesus really did feel abandoned—but it involved much more for him. . .
> **Into your hands I commit my spirit.** Yes, eventually even Jesus must come to a place of acceptance.

The words of Jesus in the throes of abandonment is just a natural human response: *"Why have you left me?"* In this secret heart-cry of many men, I find at least three powerful connections coupled with certain sad potentialities in a man's development.

"There must be something wrong with me." The Potential for Shame. Gary says, "A few years after Dad died, I started feeling lumps in my own body. I was sure I had cancer, just like the kind that had killed my father. I remember riding the high school bus thinking: *If only I can get through this school year, or even the basketball season, then I'll be ready to die.* Such thoughts from a healthy, 17-year-old kid! I felt flawed in some way, ashamed of myself for what had happened."

"I just don't know what to do!" The Potential for Confused Decision Making. Losing a father at a young age

produces a "guidance gap". The searching son longs for affirmation, but a continuous sense of dissatisfaction with accomplishments takes over. No matter how great, those accomplishments never receive the absent father's approval, raising the false hope that perhaps the next venture will produce the desired approval from. . . somewhere.

In the abandoned son's mind, the endless questions swirl: *What should I do next? Have I been a failure so far? Why do I never feel as though I've done enough? Will I ever come to a place of peace about where I am in life?* One man I know described the guidance gap this way: "I wish I could have just once heard these words from my father before he died: 'Son, I'm so very proud of you.' I think then I could have learned to relax a little in life; sit back and enjoy the ride a little more."

"I'll never let things get so bad again!" The Potential for Controlling Behavior. Many men who've had out-of-control family situations growing up begin to believe, "If I can just keep bad things from happening from now on, I'll be okay." The problem manifests itself in how we relate to our families. We end up alienating them as we try to design and control our own futures, make our children turn out just right, build a career path that won't disappoint and produce a world of satisfaction for ourselves. In the process, we lose out on the ways God could gift us with gracious surprises, if we would just loosen our grip a bit.

Pastoring the Father-Wounded Man

Pastoring men with the father wound means allowing them to re-experience their grief when it bubbles up, being with them in their sadness for their own abandonment. Help them acknowledge their longing for what they *really* want: the unconditional love and acceptance

that flows only from the Father God. Help them move away from substitutes (addictive escapes) for that love.

Opportunities for such pastoring come when you become known among your men as a person of unconditional love and total commitment to the other man's agenda. You'll *commit to listening with your heart* in those moments when a man opens up and statements like these from you will be helpful:

- "How is that for you, Joe?" (Now listen, listen, listen. . .)
- "What are the tears, brother?" (Now listen. . .)
- "That must hurt." (Listen. . .)
- "So you're feeling the pain of it now?" (Listen. . .)

*****

Pastoral Opportunities in the Mainline Church: Invite older men of wisdom and maturity into a mentoring process with younger guys who've been left behind by their biological fathers through death, divorce, or abandonment. Provide the information, inspiration and training the older men need for this calling. Many young boys in single-mom homes need "surrogate fathers" too.

On the cross, Jesus cried, "Into thy hands I commit my spirit." These words speak of the movement toward acceptance—and even an ability to gain from the experience of loss. Even though the absence of a father is a wound a boy carries forever, it does not have to be a deadly wound, grievously sidetracking us on our spiritual journey. Instead, the "search for Dad" can gradually take us up onto the road that leads toward acceptance.

HEART CRY #2: "Challenge me with a great cause!"

I call this the BHAJ—the BIG, HOLY, AUDACIOUS JOURNEY. Some men have been stuck in the foothills for life, when their heart's desire has always been to climb to the top of the mountain, even against impossible odds. Yet, in the church, they have often found a hodgepodge of undifferentiated programs and activities—no direction, no journey, no mountain. In many cases our highest level of spiritual calling for men has been to be an usher.

We are talking about *the benign neglect of men here!* We have created a *gap* that says either go all out for God (and head off to seminary immediately) or settle for the small-challenge role (be an usher, greeter, etc.).

Now I have served as an usher and it is a vital ministry role in our churches. But my point is there was no calling up to a high vision—up to what our hearts desire. Daniel Moore writes in *Warrior Wisdom:* "We are still warriors of one kind or another, called upon to match daring with expertise. Business competition and the search for satisfying, self-affirming jobs can be just as treacherous as navigating through a bay of pirates. The dangers just seem smaller because today's bad guys have more social polish than their earlier counterparts—and better suits."[3]

If men are challenged like that in the *daily* life of the business world, isn't the call of the Great Commission even more compelling, in that it deals with *eternal* life and death? If we refuse to challenge men as Jesus did, then we are politely neglecting their deepest longings.

STORY FROM THE MISSION FIELD

JAY CROUSE

In January of 2004, at our annual Diocese of Southwest Florida's Episcopal Men's Ministries leadership team meeting with our bishop, John Lipscomb, the bishop had a surprise announcement. He had a vision about where God needed us to invest our time. It was a radical vision, one that would take us out of our comfort zone. The bishop's vision was to equip Christian men in southwest Florida to be prepared to disciple 1,000 new men of faith.

His vision became known as Equipping the 70 and included the following parameters: that our leadership team become ecumenical; that our model for equipping men focus on three spiritual disciplines: sharing our faith, defending our faith, and discipling; and that our model be based on Luke 10:1-12, 17.

Now this was a serious challenge. Where to begin? We started with a dictionary in order to look up the word "ecumenical"! Our leadership team, since our inception, had been a regionally based, denominational (Episcopal) group. The bishop's first request was that we expand our team to include men of other denominations and nondenominational churches. That one step proved to be significant in itself as we came to represent the church of Jesus Christ in southwest Florida.

In addition to needing to expand our team, we faced other challenges. We had no plan or existing model to follow; we did not have qualified faculty to teach the three spiritual disciplines; and, finally, we did not have the financial resources to implement this vision. We quickly learned that for what God ordains, He provides the resources to succeed.

Our expanded team began to put the puzzle pieces together. We developed an equipping model that included three day-long courses focused on each of the three spiritual disciplines: sharing our faith, defending our faith and discipling. Then we contracted with three leading specialists to teach each of these three courses: Fr. Charles Fulton, Fr. Jerry Smith and Phil Downer. Finally, through the passion of my friend, Tom Riley, we were blessed to receive a grant from the Encourage, Inc. Christian Foundation to meet all of our financial needs.

We then launched the initiative, Equipping the 70, in January 2005 with a call to men throughout southwest Florida to be equipped to disciple one thousand new men of faith. "The 70" showed up and much was expected of them. These men were required to attend each of the three, day-long spiritual discipline equipping courses; talk with their pastor about their involvement and provide a signed commitment form from their pastor; invite another person to serve as their prayer partner through the duration of the course; attend a weekend releasing conference; and, when released, to go out two by two (Luke 10:1) into the mission field to disciple 1,000 new men of faith.

Over a four-year period, our challenging, men's ministry initiative equipped 125 men as disciple makers. Those 125 men were then sent out, two by two, to disciple 1,000 new men of faith. Men did and will respond to a clear spiritual vision that is communicated by a respected leader with a big goal, a defined plan and a challenge that stirs their hearts.

Pastoring Men in the Gap

Pastoring men who face the limited choice of seminary or ushering requires a full immersion in spiritual gift discovery. You'll need to search out a good curriculum to guide

167

you here and then invite a man to learn with you: (1) every Christian is given at least one spiritual gift at baptism; (2) every Christian is responsible to discover and use his gifts in ministry in the church to edify other believers and so help build up the body of Christ; (3) every gift is of supreme importance in the church—and Jesus places men in the church, with their particular mix of gifts, as a way of keeping His body well balanced and healthy so that it can reach out to the lost effectively; and (4) *fully exercising one's spiritual gifts is the greatest adventure journey on earth!*

Recommended resource for gift discovery:

Discover Your Spiritual Gifts the Network Way, by Bruce Bugbee. This is a total program for individuals and groups, complete with inventories for gift identification.

*****

Pastoral Opportunities in the Mainline Church: Stop being purely a "maintenance operation". From its beginning, the church was a missionary entity. As men learn and exercise their spiritual gifts through your pastoral teaching and coaching, challenge them with the goal of launching salt-and-light forays into a pagan world. *They* are to be that salt and light! Show them how and train them how. It's more than signing up for a committee—it's transformation.

When it comes to challenging a man at the heart level, my friend Fr. Lance Wallace puts it like this: "We know from Romans 12 that you've got to have your head changed. Your *thoughts* must be converted before you can change your behavior. Men have to see that and go, *Oh, I'm not* acting *the way I should!* It's a rational thing, but in the meantime you must have your heart softened. And that's a spiritual thing that happens through the sacraments, I believe."

HEART CRY #3: "Give me a solid friend—and a group of brothers in support!"

Many men are relationally isolated while secretly longing for long-term friendships. In a recent study conducted by Promise Keepers, men were asked how they would deal with a crisis in their family or job. Would they turn to Christian friends for assistance and advice, or would they deal with it in some other way? "We discovered that a minority of men—42%—said they would turn to Christian friends. These data suggest that even though men have what they consider to be close Christian friends in place, those relational networks do not typically get used effectively."[4]

A deep friendship implies a level of intimacy that is rare for men. Kevin McClone, in his article on "male intimacy" writes, "At best men are friendly, rather than intimate, in their relationships. . . it seems much easier for men to share activities such as sports rather than their inner selves."[5]

STORY FROM THE MISSION FIELD

HAL HADDEN

Can you believe 12 high-powered businessmen would commit to meeting for two years, one morning a week before work, and come to the meeting with their lessons prepared? With that long-term commitment, men are willing to connect on not only the head level, but the heart level as well. Let me give you an example that I experienced.

One morning Robert was running late and I suggested we rib him a bit, as men like to do, by telling him that it was his turn to bring breakfast and he must have forgotten it. We expected an embarrassed chuckle, but instead heard Robert say, "My daughter died last night." It blew us away.

We knew Robert's daughter had been critically ill, as we had been getting reports and we had been praying for her and listening to our friend in his sad time. Yet, this day, we didn't know how to respond. We were speechless. We cried with Robert, prayed with him, hugged him and stared into space, hoping someone could come up with some way to lift the heaviness we were all feeling. We really did connect with Robert on a level that we, as men, had never connected before. We had shared our stories, talked about biblical passages, discussed contemporary Christian books on leadership, business, family and our relationship with God, but we had kept things on the surface, especially the matters of our hearts.

That is what men do. We love a challenge, we love to share our ideas and we love to get on with the game plan, but we don't like to get into feelings or to the very core of our being: the heart. Someone once said in another group that I was leading that he "wanted to put on his skirt", meaning he was getting ready to share his feelings and heart. I encouraged him to share the situation, but did suggest that although men don't wear skirts, God did make us with feelings and even tender hearts and we can share with those willing to accept us right where we are and stand with us for the long haul.

This is what these men experienced. When we met the next week, after the funeral, we asked Robert why he had even come to the meeting that morning because he had every reason to miss it, especially since he was flying that same day to the northeast, where his daughter had been living. He told us he actually had a flight booked that was scheduled to leave during our meeting, but changed it because he "needed his buddies to stand with him and prepare him for the heavy emotional week to come."

It has been eight years since our group ended and when asked what the most impactful part of the experience was without exception, the 11 of us would say standing with Robert and learning what God was teaching us through this painful experience. We were given the opportunity to hear Robert's heart and to empathize and care for him. We learned this during the months leading up to his daughter's death, the week of her death, the funeral and the reality of loss in the months and years that followed. This wasn't part of the course curriculum, but it was in God's curriculum for us. He was teaching us how to move from always operating with our heads and our to-do lists to actually hearing and responding to our friend's feelings. God taught us to identify our feelings and even express them in tears, prayers, hugs, silence and maybe a word of encouragement, never cheap advice or Bible-bullet. It felt right to live out who God created us to be.

Pastoring the Isolated Man

Remember the importance of indirection. Since men build relationships best when they are focused on working on some project or activity together, initiate activities that have nonthreatening "entry points". ABI = Always Be Inviting. Be on the lookout for that man who needs a friend; invite him into your church, your group, your life.

*****

Pastoral Opportunities in the Mainline Church: Church of the Redeemer in Sarasota, Florida, for instance, holds regular steak dinners, spring baseball outings, golf outings, Christmas shopping nights and Valentine dinners with spouses.

The list for your church could go on and on, limited only by the creative imaginations of your men's planning team. The entry points lead to relationship-building events, where lasting friendships form. *But remember: healthy relationships among men, not programs, are the goal*

Some guys will say that "relationships" are for women. True, as we've seen, men don't naturally think of "relationship" as a goal. But they do need close friends, nonetheless. Pastoring in the context of men's ministry requires us leaders to help them here. The mighty King David uttered these words: "I grieve for you, Jonathan my brother; you were very dear to me. Your love for me was wonderful, more wonderful than that of women" (2 Samuel 1:26). Now that's a close relationship in the life of a great biblical role model!

HEART CRY #4: "Deliver me from my addictions!"

Many men unconsciously sense the need to fill a hole in their soul! Think back to the father wound. An absent father, for instance, produces a gaping, yawing "hole in the soul" that won't ever be completely filled this side of glory. I've come to see, through long experience, that this insatiable chasm can be made smaller only by being inside it and drawing it inward, rather than trying to satisfy it with any number of mood-altering fixes: food, relationships, work, pornography, drugs—the standard ways to medicate this inner pain.

As we men allow ourselves to re-experience our grief when it bubbles up, we can expect that it will move us to greater

Can You Pastor Their Hearts?

---

awareness of what we *really* want: the unconditional love and acceptance that flows from God, our Father in heaven.

Pastoring the Addicted Man

Pastoring the addicted is all about leading them into their pain. That's right: *into* it, not away from it. They are already experts at running away, which is the essence of addiction: an escape, a medication, a substitute for the legitimate suffering of real hurts and griefs of the past.

So get them into accountability groups in your church and in other venues, such as Alcoholics Anonymous or Sexaholics Anonymous. But don't assume that willpower alone can cure addictions. It can't. In fact, willpower feeds addiction. Only by the full grieving of deep woundedness can a man ultimately find relief from internal compulsions. It may take years of going back and back again, to the painful situations and connecting them to the genuine emotions that were once too scary to face head on.

All of this assumes two things: (1) Jesus is the Great Physician and must be the power behind every cure and (2) Jesus is the indwelling presence who will take the place of the addiction and fill that "hole in the soul" with a relationship that is more satisfying than the relationship with the medication of choice. As someone has said, "You can only fight the darkness by bringing in the light." Men don't overcome addictions by fighting them so much as by moving toward something that is more compelling, the Lord God of all!

*****

- *Pastoral Opportunities in the Mainline Church:* Develop key leaders who are well versed in the nature and practice of forming accountability relationships among men. Additionally, a church should make sure it makes trained spiritual directors available for men and know when and how to refer them for professional counseling.

The apostle Paul apparently struggled with some form of besetting sin, or addiction. He wrote,

> *For what I am doing, I do not understand. For what I will to do, that I do not practice; but what I hate, that I do... What a wretched man I am!* (Romans 7:15, 24)

The hopeful side to any story of a man who has reached "rock bottom" with his addictions is this: that is the very point at which he can make spectacular change for the better. I love how C. S. Lewis once put it: "God, who has made us, knows what we are and that our happiness lies in him. Yet we will not seek it in him as long as he leaves us any other resort where it can even plausibly be looked for. While what we call 'our own life' remains agreeable, we will not surrender it to him."[6]

HEART CRY #5: "Give me something or someone to honor, serve, thank and praise."

This one may seem unusual, but let me tell you about Stan. We were sitting in a small group discussing the question: "How did you come to be Jesus's follower?" A couple of the guys told stories about reaching "rock bottom" in their lives and needing a Savior. Some of them were literally down and out, others had been quite successful from all appearances, but they suffered a hunger for "something more" in life that would save them from self-destructive habits or dysfunctional relationships.

Stan was different. He told a story of reaching midlife with a satisfying sense of accomplishment. Things were good at home and in his hardware store business and had been for as long as he could remember. In fact, his life—always free of any kind of church involvement—had been blessed down through the years, surprisingly trouble-free and filled with good times. His response? "I reached a point where I really started wanting something or someone *to thank!*"

Pastoring the Contented Man

This one should be fairly obvious. You will have many interactions with men who seem to have it all together and who are, to a large degree, content with their lives. However, the words of St. Augustine continue to ring true down through the ages: "Our hearts are restless until they rest in Thee."

All this man needs is a few gentle reminders to pursue his desire to offer gratitude, to find out exactly Who is behind the grace that's been poured into his life. Get him into Bible studies and small groups and bring him into contact with other guys who are not so content, guys facing tough circumstances. This man's heart is waiting to be pierced with compassion. It will happen as you shepherd him into interacting with the full spectrum of life's challenges.

*****

Pastoral Opportunities in the Mainline Church: Make sure your church's worship is, indeed, directed toward God as a means of saying, "Thank You!" We can easily move away from adoring the King of the universe who holds us in His hands. That's when our focus turns to merely meeting our needs or getting something out of the service. But let us enter worship with the hope that our Lord God will be the one to get something out of it. We are the actors; He is the audience. Worship, at its best, is a joy we render to our Lord, beyond an experience we hope to receive.

This powerful urge to give thanks to whatever it was in the universe that seemed to be blessing him was the impetus for Stan to "check out" what was happening at the church closest to his home. He took his family, too and the rest, as they say, is history.

We've come to the end of Part 2 of this book, surveying five areas in which we can work at welcoming men back to the church. Having considered what the welcomed man would need to find in the church, it is now time, in Part 3, to consider the bright portrait of the churched man. In other words, what would be the practical "end product" of our efforts to secure a future in the church for men?

Your Next-Step Action Plan

CHECK YOUR OWN ADDICTIONS. It goes without saying that it is tough to help another man with his addictions if we're in the throes of addiction ourselves. If this is you, make a solid plan, without delay. Begin by finding an accountability partner and laying it on the line with him about where you are with this struggle. Or go to your priest for sacramental confession, then ask advice about where to get good counseling or group help for the long haul. Determine to stay accountable; secrecy feeds addictions.

For Personal Reflection

1. What is my past and current relationship with my father (whether he's living or dead)?

2. What wounds do I have from my father and how have I sought healing?

3. What have I learned from this chapter about how to minister to hurting men?

4. What is my "besetting sin" (or major addiction)? Do I have an accountability relationship that helps me deal with this?

For Group Discussion

1. Take turns sharing how you have been blessed—or not—by your earthly father.

2. Do you agree that most men can point to some kind of father wound? Discuss some of the effects of this woundedness in men.

3. As discussed in the preface, what is meant by the benign neglect of men? How is the ministry "gap" related to this?

4. Talk about the problem of addictions among Christian men. As you are comfortable doing so, share together about your own struggles. Pray for one another and promise confidentiality.

5. Discuss each opportunity for the mainline church from this chapter and assess your own church's readiness to help men with their heart-cries in each area.

PART III

A BLESSED HOPE:
The Churched Man

Chapter 11

Blessed through His Chosen Denomination

I see the church historically separated into groups that agree on many larger issues but often vehemently disagree on smaller ones. I looked into several controversies in Christian history and found that a different way of relating to God—a way hinted at through a spiritual temperament—was behind many of them.

—Gary Thomas [1]

I believe no man should have to hear this: "Church is great and all, Tom, but you'll need to find more than that to be a serious follower of Jesus."

In other words, I'd hate to think that Tom, who sits in the pews of St. Swithin's every Sunday, would have a chance for solid spiritual formation only if he were to find a good *parachurch* ministry—a specific programming ministry that comes alongside, but is not part of a church—as his primary Christian community. With that in mind, I'll state my thesis for this chapter right up front: Men can be formed in denominational churches; they don't need to leave their denominations in order to be "parachurched" into Christian maturity.

How do I know this? Because men are wired in different ways spiritually and the denominational distinctives offer all kinds of spiritualities, particular ways of approaching God and growing in fellowship with Him. These serve as inviting doors of entrance to all kinds of men. Let me say that again, as clearly as I can: *your denomination has a few special doors that certain kinds of men will enter because of who they are.* Men need mainline churches. You need to meet them there with welcoming arms.

I've already said that the men in the pews of our churches are our "prime targets". They are our immediate market for men's ministry, even before we try to reach unchurched men. So, let's meet and begin discipling the men right there in our pews.

More to the point, they are there, in your particular denomination, for an important reason. One or more "denominational distinctives" have drawn them, at least with a surface appeal, because they meet these men at the place of their own spiritual temperament.

Particularly, I'm thinking of the mainline or denominational church. We've been "para-churched" aplenty — and that's good, but it's not enough. Why? Because the denominational church, the local body of Christ, is the only place where we can experience the sacraments and other things like. . .

Spiritual Direction
Calendar of the Church Year
Prayer for the Dead
Saints Days
Prayer Books and Missals
Silence and Solitude
Choral Traditions
Church Fathers
Apostolic Successors

**Contemplative Prayer
Solemn High Mass
Incense and Holy Water
Spirit-Filled Ceremonial and Ritual, and
Architecture as a key component of worship. . .**

. . .and much, much more that comes to us primarily in the mainline churches. We can't get all of this through any parachurch ministry.

If we are *saved* by grace and can be *sanctified* only by grace, then we must go where we find the *means* of grace: the church and its sacraments. Yet we know that only about 30% of men in America are significantly involved *in the life of a local congregation.* Of those who are inspired by the call to intentional Christian discipleship, many feel they must find their path to growth in parachurch organizations alone. In other words, for them, the local church offers no formation, no process, no mission, no challenge.

That's got to change. And if we begin working with them, right in our mainline churches, we'll find many men who discover within themselves that they want to hear and respond to the Lord's call right there. As hearts open to God, spiritual desire emerges. That's how it always is.

Yes, even with all the myriad parachurch ministry resources available to them—all the conferences, training programs, books, tapes, speakers, retreats—there is no replacing a man's local church. That is where we will actually lead men *through a process of Christian formation.*

Let's think a little more about this idea of different "kinds of men" and why we find them in different denominations. Let's consider how "spiritual temperaments" look in individuals and how denominations tend to fall into the grid. I'll do a brief survey, relying heavily on sources by three important Christian writers—Gary Thomas, Myra Perrine and Kenneth Swanson—to unfold the theory.[2] But the point is for you, a leader in your mainline church, to make the best use of your own denomination's spiritual temperament. It should help you better understand the men in your pew as you call them to the mission of Jesus in ways that resonate with their deepest selves.

One Size *Doesn't* Fit All

What is a spiritual temperament? Gary Thomas, an evangelical Baptist pastor, writer and seminary professor, speaks of nine sacred pathways—each of them being a "unique way that an individual interacts with God." In this context, it is *a man's particular predisposition for approaching and relating to God.* Of the nine, one is usually predominant in any given man.

A spiritual temperament—or "God Language", as author Myra Perrine calls it—is the *primary* way an individual finds the most meaningful or best way to approach the relationship with almighty God in worship and prayer. Perrine's book, *What's Your God Language?* which is based on Gary Thomas's original work in *Sacred Pathways,* helps us see that each temperament shows forth some aspect of God's inherent nature. As Perrine puts it,

> **Each spiritual temperament displays a distinct aspect of God's character—His justice, His care, His beauty and His changelessness. Together we are like a diamond, each showing the world a distinct facet of who God is through our unique expressions of love for Him. It's almost as if God has many "love languages." His heart is moved when each of us speaks to Him in the language of the heart, whether that be quiet meditation or robust song or speaking out against tyranny to defend the poor. Each language thrills God's heart a bit differently.[3]**

The key point is that ministry to men is not a one-size-fits-all spirituality. That's why we need the denominations. Men connect with God differently.

There's an old sermon illustration that tells of an octogenarian medical doctor prescribing penicillin for every disease he encountered. Or, as the saying goes, to the man with a hammer in his hand, everything is a nail.

As men's leaders, let's not be that man.

Here's a simple example. Many of us evangelicals grew up with the idea that having a consistent daily quiet time, with Bible reading and prayer, defined our level of spirituality. Some of us really took to that and carried the practice through into adulthood. Others, however, soon got bored with the daily routine. However, leaving the quiet time behind meant, in our circles, backsliding as a Christian. So we kept trying and trying and failing and failing. There just wasn't any other way to "be spiritual".

But why should everyone be expected to worship God the same way? Shouldn't we men's ministry leaders beware of narrowing men's options for approaching God?

I'm going to tell you more about "Don" in the next chapter. [4] But for now, let me briefly introduce him as a thoughtful, 39-year-old CPA living in Colorado, who is starting to open his heart to God. After our in-person conversation at a men's conference I led, he sent me an email response to a question I'd posed.

Here was my question:

Don, why is a liturgical and sacramental church (such as the Roman Catholic, Anglican, Episcopal traditions) appealing to you (as opposed to a free church, like Baptist, with contemporary music, etc.)?

Here was his reply:

There are several parts to my answer, I guess. I'm not as comfortable singing in church, probably one of the reasons I've gravitated to Rite 1 service in the Book of Common Prayer at the Eucharist. I believe my feelings about singing have more to do with keeping focused than any concerns about my voice (although that is a small part of it). When I sing, I'm worrying as much about what notes I should be trying for and the pacing as I am about the message of the hymn. For the same reason, while I have told Fr. Morris that I am willing and able to assist with Communion, anointing and serving during the Tuesday morning services, I prefer to stay in the congregation and listen to the words rather than worry about when to ring the bell or prepare the altar. I do like to read, though.

I believe the formality of the *Book of Common Prayer*, regardless of which Rite, allows me to focus on God without distractions—and it gives me some of the words I need, but have trouble finding on my own. For example, my private prayers tend to be brief and to the point, occasionally followed by a mental reminder of what to include, exclude, or adapt for next time. I did notice this morning, when Fr. Morris accidentally missed a small section while preparing for Communion, that I was not the only one saying to myself "Lamb of God that takest away the sins of the world."

As a kid, the churches I attended were usually Church of Christ (that's where my grandparents worshiped), but I haven't felt a strong pull that way.

Bottom line: I don't know if I'd be at St. Luke's if there wasn't a Tuesday morning mass. I try to attend a weekend mass when I can, but that seems to be maybe once a month, mostly because of my work schedule. I have looked at other churches to find out more about them, even other Episcopal churches, but none had the flexibility or opportunity for me to worship that St. Luke's does.

Your friend,

Don

Of course, there are plenty of guys who started in liturgical churches and then journeyed the other way. They ended up in free churches and could tell similar stories with different themes. So let's look at the specifics of the spiritual temperaments, as given by Thomas and Perrine and consider their influence. *Remember that they do overlap to some extent.* I'll chart them here and append a few key words and phrases that should give you an idea of what type of man gravitates to a particular temperament.[5]

THE INTELLECTUAL—loving God through the mind; knowing, understanding concepts, gaining insight; searching for truth; knowing the biblical text; memorizing Scripture; studying theology; doing philosophical or scientific inquiry; knowing the catechism; exploring church history, apologetics, ethics, doctrine; knowing the creeds.

Aspects of men's ministry that would appeal to the Intellectual: attending classes, seminars, workshops and Bible studies that seriously delve into the biblical text or other religious topics; responding to the "challenge" of studying, analyzing and synthesizing concepts for presenting to a men's gathering; having the opportunity to teach other men.

THE ACTIVIST—confronting evil on behalf of God; seeking justice for all; standing up for righteousness in hostile places; bold preaching and teaching; organizing for action; emulating the prophets; being spiritually nourished through the battle; feeling frustrated by apathy.

Aspects of men's ministry that would appeal to the **Activist:** *participating in boycotts, protest marches, or ad campaigns to confront a societal evil or advance a kingdom cause, hearing bold and prophetic teaching and preaching, attending workshops on current events and the church's role in society, getting out to organize others and "do something to make a difference", taking mission trips to do feeding or construction or other forms of helping transform a community, having political influence as a Christian.*

THE ASCETIC—loving God through solitude and simplicity; going apart, being alone, retreat, simple living, giving away, strict austerity, discipline, "beating my body into submission"; avoiding opulence, frugality; silence, self-sacrifice, and self-denial; acts of devotion, shutting out the senses, listening for God.

Aspects of men's ministry that would appeal to the **Ascetic:** *attending prayer and study groups that meet very early in the morning, being accountable for a challenging program of discipleship or training, having a mentor that can be "hard on him", not afraid to confront him in helping him leave sin behind.*

THE CAREGIVER—loving God through loving and serving others; mercy and compassion for the poor; hands-on gentleness, moved to tears by the plight of sufferers, patience and courage in a context of difficulty, able to listen to complaints with understanding, hearing moans and crying with a high level of acceptance, acquainted with grief, inviting tears of others, "staying with" the pain of others, taking on a "lost cause", doing what helps ease the pain of the deeply troubled.

Aspects of men's ministry that would appeal to the **Caregiver:** *attending major events that meet to help others: a rally day at church to prepare school backpacks to give* *to underprivileged students returning to school; serving at soup kitchens, bread ministry, food pantries; serving on a team of guys that visits hospitals or nursing homes; getting involved in prison ministry, being on a lay Eucharistic visitor team of men who take communion to the sick and homebound, reading to the blind, tutoring inner-city kids, any form of caregiving for the physically or mentally challenged, coaching youth sports or Special Olympic teams as a ministry of the church men, providing any form of hospitality: working on the breakfast team with other guys for church fellowship hour after services, being a healing prayer minister, anointing with oil and laying hands on others for prayer after they receive communion.*

THE CONTEMPLATIVE—loving God through adoration; holding hands with God; stilling the mind, emptiness; no abstractions or concepts, getting thoughts out of the way, unitive experience, direct contact with God; loving gaze; icons, candles, bells, sitting in stillness; enjoying God; basking in belovedness, attention to breathing; intimacy with the Father, desire and longing; leaving the world behind, practicing the Presence.

Aspects of men's ministry that would appeal to the Contemplative: attending Advent and Lenten Quiet Days with small groups of men of the church—each group spends some time in silence together; going on a silent retreat for men, guided by instruction beforehand; participating in any form of retreat, especially those that build in times to walk the Stations of the Cross in quietness, or to participate in individual or group centering prayer; having access, through the men's ministry, to spiritual directors and confessors provided for your men—ongoing and at special events and retreats.

THE ENTHUSIAST—loving God through mystery and celebration; "let go and let God"; enthusiastic singing and celebration in worship; experiencing God in excitement and awe; seeking the supernatural; hunger for the transcendent; intense spiritual desire; feeling fed by experience; hoping God will show up in worship; evidence of God's moving; dreams and visions; miracles of healing; great expectancy; moving with the Holy Spirit; lifting hands in praise.

*Aspects of men's ministry that would appeal to the **Enthusiast**: contemporary worship; praying for one another with faith and expectancy—especially for healing and other serious difficulties; coming to hear charismatic guest speakers; studying about the Holy Spirit; being allowed to exercise one's spiritual gifts in the ministry.*

THE NATURALIST—experiencing God outdoors; watching; listening to nature; seeing mountains, oceans, clouds; feeling the mystery and power of natural forces, as God's handiwork.

*Aspects of men's ministry that would appeal to the **Naturalist**: camping trips, fishing outings, overnight retreats, "walk and talk" for a one-to-one discipleship meeting.*

THE SENSATE—loving God through the five senses; in the presence of beauty; icons and art; classical music or jazz; glorious architecture; shaping, painting, molding; feeling God's presence in the body; cinematic masterpieces; cooking—and food, truly savored as a blessing from God.

*Aspects of men's ministry that would appeal to the **Sensate**: attending film nights—good cinema with powerful points to make and to discuss; enjoying any event that is directed toward the senses rather than to the mind and thinking; participating in activities that get men off the couch and into being active.*

THE TRADITIONALIST—loving God through ritual and symbol and sacrifice; high liturgy; glorious worship; exalted language of the prayer book or missal; relishing—and being involved in—solemn processions, choral masses, chanting psalms.

Aspects of men's ministry that would appeal to the Traditionalist: making traditional worship a standard part of your meetings; taking field trips to shrines and holy places with architecture that inspires; going on a Holy Land pilgrimage with part of the agenda being to worship in several liturgical venues: Orthodox, Roman, Anglican, Coptic, etc.; letting the men know in advance, on retreats, that you'll be saying the Daily Office together from the Book of Common Prayer or observing the Liturgy of the Hours; closing your retreat with Holy Eucharist.

If your group is largely non-liturgical or free church, developing a ritual or two that symbolizes what is happening at your retreat; having any symbolic action that kicks off, or sums up, any men's ministry event; assigning worship roles to those who revel in the ritual and symbol; for example, suppose you had a foot washing invitation after a planned event stressing unity of purpose and mutual servanthood?

Why is an understanding of the spiritual temperaments so important to men's ministry? Consider this quip that is fairly common in discussions of evangelism: "If Denny's were the only restaurant in town, would more people eat at Denny's, or would fewer people eat out?" The point is that surely fewer people would eat out; thus, we need more options if the eating-out crowd is going to swell in numbers. Here's the situation, stated in another and more negative way.

Roman Catholics, Lutherans, Calvinists, Anabaptists, and Orthodox were trying to love God, but with unique expressions of that love.

190

Many differences had theological roots, but some were also related to worship preferences...Instead of learning from others, Christians have often chosen to segregate themselves by starting a new church whenever worship preferences diverge. This segregation has erected denominational walls and impoverished many Christians. Unless you happen to be born into just the right tradition, you're brought up to feed on somebody else's diet. Unfortunately, some Christians have a tendency to question the legitimacy of any experience that may not particularly interest them. Instead of saying, "That's not for me," they proclaim, "That shouldn't be for anybody."[6]

Church: A Good Thing

Let's take a breather and remember two bottom-line truths, supported by the statistics.

Church is good for men

- Churchgoers are more likely to be married and express a higher level of satisfaction with life. Church involvement is the most important predictor of marital stability and happiness.[7]
- Church involvement moves people out of poverty. It's also correlated with less depression, more self-esteem and greater family and marital happiness.[8]
- Religious participation leads men to become more engaged husbands and fathers.[9]
- Teens with religious fathers are more likely to say they enjoy spending time with dad and that they admire him.[10]

191

Men are good for the church

A study from Hartford Seminary found that the presence of involved men is statistically correlated with church growth, health and harmony. Meanwhile, a lack of male participation is strongly associated with congregational decline.[11]

When it comes to men and the church, the simple fact is that birds of a feather will flock together. They tend to gather with those of like minds. And, if they attend church, they'll be with others of similar God language.

There is nothing wrong with this! *Indeed, the denominations give us the doors of welcoming back that we are looking for.*

> **Our spiritual temperaments often determine how and where we worship and serve the Lord. Some denominations have synthesized around spiritual preferences—such as the caregiving nature of the Salvation Army or the Traditionalist value of ritual and continuity in the Anglican Church. . . Passionate spirituality looks different from church to church, depending upon the preference of its people. . . The world will never see the full expression of the Person of God without each part of the body of Christ expressing itself differently.[12]**

Over its long history, the church has developed its traditions, as the apostle Paul indicated.

> *Therefore, brethren, stand fast and hold the tradi-*
> *tions which you were taught, whether by word or our*
> *epistle.* (2 Thessalonians 2:15)

So, the differences we see in various sectors of Christianity are understandable. And the distinctives that come through in the denominations can be to our benefit as leaders of men.

Denominational Distinctives and the Circle of Piety

Kenneth Swanson, in his book *Uncommon Prayer,* speaks of the "Circle of Piety" as a way to put spiritual temperaments into just four categories: Intellectual (or Rational), Emotional, Sensual (or Sensory) and Mystical. I'll describe these below, but I also want to try an experiment with you—considering how these relate to spiritual tempera- ments and to the denominations. I believe Swanson's four quadrants are the four broad ways denominations tend to separate themselves and offer their inviting distinctives.

The final section of this chapter will suggest how denominations break down, in my opinion, under the spiri- tual pathways. I encourage you, as a denominational leader, to make the most of your denominational distinctives in reaching men with solid Christian formation.

RATIONAL PIETY—These men will be interested in the speculative side of things, wanting "solid Bible study", with theology being very important to them. They are disciplined, dutiful and sometimes morally legalistic. Intellectual/Rational Christian men focus on God as the tran- scendent Father, awesome Creator, majestic Being, almighty Lawgiver, or even the metaphysical Absolute.[13]

Examples of Denominations functioning within a Rational piety:

Reformed Church in America
Presbyterian Church in the USA
Evangelical Free Church
Lutheran Church, Missouri Synod
Southern Baptist Convention
Anglican Church in North America

Type of Man likely attracted: Intellectuals and Traditionalists

Common Denominational Distinctives:

- Knowing and memorizing the Bible text
- Coming to a "saving knowledge" of Jesus Christ
- Interest and study in the area of apologetics
- Promoting disciplined prayer and devotional life
- Stressing the deity of Christ
- Emphasis on knowing creeds and catechisms
- Emphasis on knowing founders' teachings: e.g. Luther, Calvin
- Offering study as spiritual growth avenue
- Emphasis on orderly worship

Men's Formation within these RATIONAL Distinctives

Christian Formation practices/ideas for the Intellectual man:

- Journal your day-to-day insights in your Christian walk. Keep a prayer journal or jot down notes during personal Bible study.

- Attend classes, seminars, lectures, workshops.
- Read the newspaper with a prayerful heart and let the stories move you to intercession.
- Use the penitential seasons of Advent and Lent to ramp up your personal devotion to the Lord. Sacrifice for Him in ways that make a difference. What will you do, or not do—and hope to make a year-round habit?

Christian Formation practices/ideas for the
Traditionalist man:

- Get involved in the worship at your church by serving in capacities that honor ritual and symbol. For example, volunteer to be on the acolyte or server rotation after proper training: serve as a crucifer, torchbearer, lector, or thurifer.
- Learn to chant the epistle and/or the psalm; memorize the responses, know the creeds, polish the church's brass.
- Attend special liturgies: Benediction of the Blessed Sacrament.
- Pray according to the church calendar and make a personal study of the daily saint. Thank God for this person and see what there is to emulate in him or her.
- Make a commitment to say Morning Prayer and Evening Prayer privately or with a congregation each day.
- Commit to attending or serving at daily mass.

EMOTIONAL PIETY—These men fall in the quadrant that is opposite the rational. They tend to be interested in *experience* more than ideas. Not so interested in theology, "they seek out and revel in the experiences of faith, which can be found in charismatic worship, healing ministries, revival meetings, and small 'sharing' Bible studies or prayer groups. Formal liturgies and worship services are borne as a necessary burden. They are, however, **deeply attracted to the sacred humanity of Jesus Christ,** especially as the suffering and loving Redeemer."[14]

Examples of Denominations functioning within an Emotional piety:

> Assemblies of God
> Full Gospel Fellowship
> Pentecostal Churches
> Foursquare Gospel Church
> The Free Methodist Church
> Holiness Churches

Type of Man likely attracted: Enthusiasts and Caregivers

Common Denominational Distinctives:

- Encouraging, heartfelt worship, with bodily involvement in "letting go" to fully experience joy, sadness, excitement
- Encouraging the use of the miraculous gifts, such as healing, speaking in tongues, interpreting tongues
- Offering the full gospel as found in the book of Acts, including the powerful experience of baptism of the Holy Spirit (Pentecostal/charismatic) or the "second blessing," or entire sanctification (Methodist)
- Preaching a heartfelt and emotional conversion experience
- Living by the direct leading of the Holy Spirit as you hear His voice

Men's Formation within these EMOTIONAL Distinctives

Christian Formation practices/ideas for the
Enthusiast man:

- Listen to contemporary music and pay particular attention to the words.
- Go to healing services and lay yourself before God for healing in body, mind and spirit.
- Seek every gift the Holy Spirit intends for you without trying to "force" anything at all.
- Immerse yourself in the psalms and the emotions and experiences of King David as he faced real-life situations.

Christian Formation practices/ideas for the
Caregiver man:

- Build the habit of being an encourager; as a form of devotional practice, regularly write notes of encouragement to those who need it.
- Begin the habit of making the sign of the cross on your forehead first thing in the morning, as St. Augustine did. Let this remind you to pray: "Here I am Lord, Your servant, use me to care for others this day. Lead me where You will; I am committing my steps to You this day."
- Memorize Scriptures that support and encourage your caregiving temperament, such as James 1:27.
- Pray for the spirit of uncompromising hospitality, then plan on how you can better open your home and life to others and their needs while maintaining reasonable boundaries.

- Take up a lifelong project of learning. Learn to listen with your heart. Learn to let others have their space in your presence. Learn to let another's agenda take precedence with you — you don't have to teach or change them in any way. Learn to receive them in love, without judging. This really is a lifetime project!

SENSORY PIETY (World Affirming) — Men in this quadrant experience God mainly through their senses, knowing God in the beauty and awesomeness they encounter *in the world.* "For them, prayer is linked to their senses and is focused on material objects. . . Sensory Christians **tend to be extremely sacramental**, seeing that in every way, grace perfects nature. Theologically, they champion the doctrines of Creation and the Incarnation, stressing both Jesus's sacred humanity and his role as the cosmic Christ renewing all things."[15]

Examples of Denominations functioning within a Sensory piety:

> The Roman Catholic Church
> The Episcopal Church/Anglo-Catholic churches
> The Church of the Brethren
> Mennonite Churches

Type of Man likely attracted: Naturalists, Sensates and Activists.

Common Denominational Distinctives:

- Encouraging sacramental theology or activist theology
- Emphasizing the role of habit/duty in sanctifying us
- Seeing holiness as comprising good works done for others in Jesus's name

- "Doing" in the real life of the material world
- Carrying out practical acts of mercy
- Caring for the earth, conservation, wildlife
- Appreciating scientific endeavor
- Changing the political situation
- Anabaptist: separating from the world and worldly, or fleshly values
- Pacifism: opting out of military service; alternative peace activities; choosing passive nonresistance in the face of force

Men's Formation within these SENSUAL Distinctives

Christian Formation practices/ideas for the Naturalist man:

- Find time to be outdoors with an eye to awareness of creation.
- Journal observations of your surroundings and write or say brief sentence-prayers of thanks, praise, request, or confession.
- Seek out places of "awesomeness"; take photos, sketch, or write your reactions. Ask how God is speaking to you here.
- Find a place outside to read and meditate on Scripture. Focus on knowing and feeling God's love for you.

Christian Formation practices/ideas for the Sensate man:

- Travel to an art show or art museum; sit before beautiful artworks and let their beauty seep into and nourish your soul.

- Worship in a church where you can "taste and see that the Lord is good" (Psalm 34:8) by attending the Holy Eucharist regularly. **Taste** the body and blood of Christ, **touch** your knees to the kneeler and feel healing oil on your forehead, **smell** the incense, **see** the stained glass and shining brass and glory in **hearing** the soaring notes of the pipe organ.
- Pray to the Lord by showing Him what's in your heart: drawing, painting, sculpting, building.
- Let your body pray without words: bowing, kneeling, genuflecting, crossing yourself with holy water, praying the Rosary.
- Light a candle before you pray or sit in God's presence.
- Like King David, find a time to dance before the Lord (clothed in public, of course).
- Serve him with your hands and feet in a multitude of creative ways!

Christian Formation practices/ideas for the Activist man:

- Pray regularly for justice and peace for all people, perhaps developing a prayer list of neighbors and friends who seem to be compromising with evil.
- As an act of prayer and obedience, stay current with news of the world and the "hot spots" of injustice. Pray over daily research findings.
- Study the Gospels day by day in order to see and emulate the *compassion* of Jesus in His work in the world.
- Have a regular meeting with a group that holds you accountable to justice and peace in your own decisions and daily way of life.

MYSTICAL PIETY (World Denying)—"If sensual Christians find intimacy with God through their senses, mystical Christians experience God *beyond* both their senses and intellect. They grope for a mystical, unmediated relationship with God. Material things are not seen as evil, but simply as a nuisance or hindrance to a pure encounter with God. Their path to God through the *via negativa,* is often expressed in negative terms such as the 'cloud of unknowing', the 'dark night of the soul', the desert, or the wilderness. Mystical Christians tend to focus on God the Father as holy, transcendent, and hidden, and often ignore the implications of an incarnational theology."[16]

Examples of Denominations functioning within a Mystical piety:

Religious Society of Friends (Quakers)
Eastern Orthodox churches

Type of Man likely attracted: Ascetics and Contemplatives

Common Denominational Distinctives:

- Experiencing the Holy Mysteries without words; glorying in the chanting of psalms and billowing of the smoke of incense, the beauty of vestments and architecture
- Having a theology of "divinization"—whether feeling it or not, knowing that participation in the sacraments is making one more like Christ through the impartation of and sharing in the nature of Christ by infused grace
- Using beauty in worship: architecture, icons and art, or, the "beauty of simplicity": spare meeting houses, simple living, etc.

Men's Formation within these MYSTICAL Distinctives

Christian Formation practices/ideas for the Ascetic man:

- Sign up for difficult church duty—for example, the all-night "watch" of the church's tabernacle during the Good Friday vigil. Stay awake all night and read devotional materials from St. Augustine's Prayer Book.
- Habitually practice forms of self-mortification: fasting, prayer vigils, early morning prayers, strict dieting of "healthy foods" with thankfulness to God.
- Take up a challenging Scripture memory plan or Bible reading plan—and stick to it.
- Work on stilling the mind, day by day, to hear the "still, small voice" of the Lord.
- Faithfully journal your spiritual insights, setting goals for growth. Check your progress.
- Have a regular silent retreat(s) scheduled during the year.

Christian Formation practices/ideas for the Contemplative man:

- As a daily devotional practice, light a candle and sit in silence in God's presence.
- Memorize and use the Jesus prayer as a means of stilling the mind: "Lord Jesus Christ, Son of God, have mercy on me, a sinner."
- Regularly allow God to lead your prayers, as if He were the lead dance partner. Truly "note" what God is saying as you listen for Him. Journal your experience of being in God's presence.
- Practice *awareness* as a spiritual discipline. Notice the signs in your heart, circumstances and desires as "grist" for the mill as you seek God's guidance, will

and wisdom. Practice "holy leisure" regularly—just hanging out with God.

- Practice a "secret act of devotion" as often as you can. This is doing some service or giving a gift anonymously without anyone ever knowing the benefactor.
- Use icons, statuettes, necklaces and rosaries in order to help you enter into a spirit of prayer. Remember, parachurch isn't the church, which is the body of Christ. While fellowship with our brothers is important, we need the entire body of Christ, which is composed of both men and women.

Your Way to "The Way"

Parachurch cannot be the only route for men. Yes, use parachurch materials, methods and conferences, but don't neglect the local church, in your denomination's piety, to form the men at a grassroots level, where they receive their foundational spiritual life. If we toss this out, we lose all the brothers of the first millennium who remain with us in the communion of saints. In that case, we'd have to ask: How is this, then, a true Christian fellowship?

> **A pastor said to me, "I think you've told me why pastors hear so much criticism of worship services and so little praise: a particular variety of service will only please one-ninth of Christians!" My pastor friend is right: Each church is full of conflicting temperaments. It is unreasonable to expect everyone's spiritual needs to be fully met by an hour-long service every seven days.[17]**

Your Next-Step Action Plan

TAKE YOUR SPIRITUAL TEMPERAMENT. Carefully study the descriptions of spiritual temperament, and determine where you fit in this grid. Then, choose one of the Christian formation suggestions that appeals to you and fits with your God language. Experiment with this "pathway" for a solid two weeks, keeping a journal of your prayers of petition and thanks.

For Personal Reflection

1. What is my particular God language? How does this help me understand *why* I'm a member of a particular church?

2. What is it about my denomination that I really appreciate?

3. What practices, or forms of devotion—characteristic of my denomination—can help me grow in Christ right here in my local church?

4. What parachurch organizations or programs could be helpful in supplementing my growth in Christ? (Refer to the additional resources in Appendix A.)

For Group Discussion

1. What is your group's reaction to the different views on denominations? Where do you agree or disagree? Is there anything you would add?

2. Talk together about your personal "God languages" or spiritual temperaments. What is the effect of this mix in your church and men's ministry?

3. If you had to name some of your denomination's distinctives, what would they be? What and how are they attractive to certain kinds of men?

4. How, specifically, can your denominational distinctives be directed toward men as "open doors" for them?

5. What specific traditions/spiritual practices in your denomination could help grow a man in Christian formation?

Chapter 12

Blessed in His Journey Inward: Coming Home

The hardest part of moving into mature believing is to allow oneself to be the object of God's delight.
—**Alan Jones**[1]

Let's now return to my conversation with Don, the 39-nine-year-old, divorced dad of two sons and one daughter, an accountant who was living with a new girlfriend in Colorado. He told me he had been baptized as a child, but had been mostly absent from any church involvement through the years. Yet now he was starting to go regularly to church and some things were "changing in my life, spiritually." It was great to talk with him that day and to continue the conversation by email once I returned to Florida. I asked him several questions, but I'll give you the gist of his response to just one of them here.

Question: Do you have a sense that you have reached full manhood?

"I've got about six months until I turn 40 and I'm not sure I have this figured out. The closest I can come is trying to be a good father, to raise my kids right, to be understanding, stern and fair with them all at once. I hope being a man means doing what needs to be done rather than what you want to do, but I still struggle with that."

My heart goes out to all the Dons around me. I want them to know Christ and keep growing spiritually. But the big question before me—and for any aspiring church leader of men is this: how do I see Don in a few years, after he has been heavily involved in the intentional men's Christian formation processes and programs in my church? What effect will those things have had upon him? In essence, I'm wondering, *"Do I really have a clear goal in mind for Don?"*

In other words, now that you've entered **Part 3** of this book, you'll focus on exploring the motivation for all that has come before this. Why, really, are we putting forth so much energy for men's ministry? What is it we want to see as the "end product" of our efforts?

At What Are We Aiming?

I believe we want to see a transformed man. It's a good thing to aim for, as that is exactly what Jesus aimed for! Thankfully, our Lord is the one who makes it happen. Yet He invites us to be His hands and feet in the world to accomplish this purpose.

So consider: what would Don, who has begun to respond to certain spiritual nudgings, look like if he were experiencing Christian formation through the warm welcome and discipling programs of your church? In other words, what is our goal for him? Can we picture it? Let's take up that "portrait painting" in this chapter, while learning a little bit more about Don's issues and needs.

We start with a simple theological affirmation: God takes joy in Don. Coming *to know and feel one's self as the object of God's delight* is the great challenge of a man's spiritual growth. The powerful image here is the baptism of Jesus. According to Matthew 3, as our Lord came up out of the water, the heavens opened, the Spirit of God descended upon Him, and the Father's voice rang out: "This is my beloved Son, in whom I am well pleased."

In our own baptism, through adoption, we, too have become sons of God and beloved in Christ. A Christian man, increasing in spiritual maturity, has an ever-widening capacity for living within this true identity as beloved. The church has a great future with men, if it can find ways of enthralling their hearts with this picture of themselves. I believe this work of enthrallment means inviting men into three great journeys suggested by Jesus's summary of the commandments: (1) to love **God** with all our being, and (2) to love our **neighbor,** as we (3) love our **selves** (see Matthew 22:38, 39).

A man is called to journey into deeper relation with self, God and neighbor. We'll look at each of these areas in turn, in this chapter and the two that follow—the *in*-ward, *God*-ward, and *out*-ward journey.

If Don is beginning to respond, we'll see him with a growing **open-heartedness** for self-understanding, a deepening **surrender** in his union with God, and an increasing **willingness to belong** to a community involved in mission. Sadly, we men often are estranged from our true selves, from God as the source of our deepest longings and from most everyone else. Our goal is to return men to the church with a warm welcome. This requires us, as church leaders, to help men move from alienation to wholeness.

He's Growing in Openheartedness

As Don and I continued to talk, his expression turned quite serious. . .

What's on your mind at the moment, Don?

"Well, I was just thinking that one thing to know about me is that the idea of 'home life' is a mystery to me. I ended up with both parents divorced, so just before I left home, neither of the "adults" in my house was an actual parent of mine. . . I guess it's no wonder I have trouble sticking with any one woman long enough to have my own home—seems I'm always leaving somebody—even though I've got kids of my own now."

There's some bad news in Don's story as it tumbles out. Plenty of dysfunction here. But the good news is clear to me: he is beginning to open his heart. He's looking at himself with an eye toward something better. We could say he's reached a point of pain in his life where he is willing to get off the escape route. As Swiss psychiatrist Carl Jung said, "All neurosis is an escape from legitimate suffering." But there can be an end to escaping.

Think about it: "neurosis" is a way of dealing with life that buries our pain—closes us up and armors ourselves against it—especially the nearly universal pain of the losses and abandonments of childhood. When we push that hurt down, it may recede from our consciousness, but it won't leave our bodies. So what happens? We suffer that pain *symbolically*. For example. . .

- we suffer headaches or other psychosomatic symptoms
- we suffer generalized anxiety, phobias, compulsions

- we suffer addictions to any number of substances or processes
- we suffer through dysfunctional relationships
- we suffer the effects of raging and out-of-control reactions
- we suffer poor decisions that take us from one crisis to the next

The list of symbolic sufferings could go on and on. I see this kind of suffering quite a lot as I work with men. Thankfully, I also see courageous guys in small groups or one on one, sharing about their struggles. A man will take a little foray into his inner life and then step back out for a while, talk it over with a trusted friend, then go back again. Little by little, he touches it and deals with it. Little by little the pain lessens and life gets better. His heart keeps opening. He's growing.

I knew a serious, fairly reserved guy whose jaw muscles were constantly tight. He did a lot of public speaking, but sometimes this facial tension was so great that he could barely open his mouth. What was going on? As he explored this problem with a good counselor, he began to see how much anger he'd stuffed inside over the years. Truth be told, he literally wanted to "bite" a few heads off! To face this with stark honesty—and to do something about it—was a truly painful process. For years it had been easier just to go around with clenched jaw.

The point is, when a man becomes willing to start suffering *legitimately*, he's made a major decision. He's turning to look at his authentic self. This is a key sign of spiritual growth in him and the essential starting point of the journey in masculine spirituality. He will have to allow himself to know the sadness in his life. He will begin to grieve the child he truly was and see the man he truly is. He will start to look at what is actually there, connecting his sufferings to their real source.

If there are certain tasks required to heal the masculine soul, at the top of the list, then, come these two items: to admit woundedness and to commit to examining the wounds. Our goal for Don is that he keep an open heart to *knowing himself* in this way—with eyes wide open to see what is really there. It means lifelong discovery and it will be worth it. As Philip Yancey has said, "Self exposure is never easy, but when I do it, I learn that underneath the layers of grime lies a damaged *work of art* that God longs to repair. . . the most important part of prayer may be to let our true selves *be loved by God*."[2]

It's a Homing Instinct

The portrait of Don as an openhearted man depicts him with an ever-softening stance toward his deeper longings and the source of them. As I think of Don's words about "home life", my thoughts move to the parable of the lost son. Jesus spoke of a young man filled with desire. On the surface level, he simply wanted his inheritance money. What he ended up receiving, though, was infinitely more valuable to him: the experience of deep affection from his father. It began with an intriguing turnaround.

> *"But when he had spent all, there arose a severe famine in that land, and he began to be in want. Then he went and joined himself to a citizen of that country, and he sent him into his fields to feed swine. And he would gladly have filled his stomach with the pods that the swine ate, and no one gave him anything. But when he came to himself, he said, 'How many of my father's hired servants have bread enough and to spare, and I perish with hunger!'"* (Luke 15:14-17)

He began to be in want and he "came to himself". In other words, sticking with his intense hunger long enough, he came to recognize what he *really* wanted. It's an important principle. If, in the grips of our longings, we will simply let them be while we observe them, sit with them in silence and acknowledge their pain and wonder, a deeper desire will bubble up from the depths. If we follow it, it will lead us home. I don't know who said it, but it rings true with me: "True spiritual maturity is the serious honoring of the validity of our *deepest* longings."

Of course, we've got to be careful here. Our shallow desires can certainly lead us into trouble! What I want does not always lead to what I need and it certainly doesn't always lead to God. Much of what we want to do is merely sinful.

However, I'm simply saying that if we embrace our longings long enough, they can lead us to the "source" in this sense: it is God Himself who is always calling us and He will *make use of* our inordinate affections, disordered desires, waywardness and pain-inducing attachments. In our pain we may learn to loosen our grip; the Lord even helps us pry our fingers away. Psychologist Gerald May put it like this:

> **God brings into our lives the *loss* of what we have been holding onto, what identifies us, what is "saving" our ego. We are forced to let it go and given the opportunity to just *be* in His love.** [3]

Consider how this works with sexual longings, for instance. My friend, Gary, wrote about his experience of walking into a video store years ago and feeling a pull to the "adult" section.

> **The tough part about temptation is that every form of it promises relief from some kind of**

deprivation, spiritual alienation, aloneness, or the sense that I am split off from a part of me that longs for sweet reunion. Sexual lust, especially, offers a few seemingly sacred moments of no separation. In mindless ecstasy, I become unified—pull all the fragments of my personality together, if only for a brief moment—assuming I will never wake up.

But the waking comes so immediately; then the shame, the guilt, and the stark re-entry of longing. And the cycle of temptation starts another round.

One thing that's helped me is to begin viewing "sin" in a different light—not as something I steel myself against when temptation hits, but as something I finally gain the *freedom* not to do, as I recognize its self-destructive effects.

I do hunger for comfort in my loneliness. Yet I must be careful not to feed the hunger without continuing to go back to the pain that causes it. Otherwise I keep hoping to fill that "gap" in me with things that won't satisfy it.

No doubt the best way out is this: to look steadily at what is being offered and to ask, calmly, *Is this what I* really *want?* In the times when I risk letting that question sink in, I sometimes sense a deeper need beneath my desire for the bright, shiny object so temptingly offered. The object of my temptation works insidiously to keep me from thinking, to keep me from feeling, to keep me at a distance from the true desires of my heart. Yes, then temptation begins to show its true colors: a mindless detour on the path to authentic fulfillment in the Lord.[4]

Priest and writer Alan Jones says that the unmaking of a soul depends on how far it refuses to follow its own homing instinct.[5] Therefore, our goal for Don is that his ever-opening heart keeps leading him toward home, the realm of his heavenly Father. We can help him see that examining his deepest desires—not running from them, but lifting them before God—can lead to soul-healing peace and joy. Radical turnarounds have a way of doing that.

> *And he arose and came to his father. But when he was still a great way off, his father saw him and had compassion, and ran and fell on his neck and kissed him.* (Luke 15:20)

A masculine spirituality just can't avoid the "I *want*". We men are creatures of prolific, bountiful desire. On television I see "Tim, the Tool Man" making a list of all the latest Binford tools he'd love to crank into action. As I sit writing this, I feel the surging juices of my own teeming desires.

> *I want to eat.*
> *I want to have sex.*
> *I want to create/build something beautiful.*
> *I want to feel my own power.*
> *I want to compete and win.*
> *I want to take a wild adventure.*
> *I want to do the impossible and heroic.*
> *I want to give and receive love.*
> *I want to offer something valuable to the world.*
> *I want to know happiness, peace, perfection.*
> *I want, want, want—even after I'm dead!—to leave a legacy.*

I want! The beauty of all this longing is that what I *really* want, I have in Christ. And if I'm asked why a "masculine" spirituality, the answer is right here in the kind of wanting I find in myself. It's all there in my body. Our male bodies have hormones and energies that women don't have. We aren't genderless beings on the earth. And men have a *particular* way of living in this world and of seeking the next world. Suppose we, in the church, were to recognize the value of a masculine spirituality that appreciates what men's bodies tell them. For example, sticking with the theme of sexuality, consider the following.

LOINS: we *want* to have sex. Our word "sex" comes from the Latin *secare*, meaning "to cut" or "separate". Our longing is to put back together what's been split off, what ought to be joined. We want loins that thrust and generate for that purpose.

EYES: we *want* to be held in eyes of love. In turn, we are stimulated by the visual. One psychotherapist tells of a study of men viewing pornography with the test givers digitally tracking eye movements. They found that those who were addicted always looked first and lingered much longer upon, the *eyes* of the woman. The point is, we long for unconditional acceptance, unreserved regard, coming through another's eyes.

CHEST: we *want* a chest bursting with appreciation of beauty. We want a chest filled with the inspiration to a grand project, especially the heroic call to rescue any loveliness in distress.

HANDS: we *want* to touch and be touched — and to be "washed" in cleansing waters. Jesus used His hands to make mud out of dirt and saliva. Then He touched a man's eyes with it. But we are armored. We also want hands that can fight and win.

GUTS: we WANT what the Bible calls "bowels of compassion". We want visceral stimulation and gutsy propositions. We want to hunt and ride fast and watch a horror movie. We want to be *moved,* which takes us down righteous and sometimes sinful pathways.

We come back to a growing openheartedness—to all his *wanting*—as a goal for Don. "All men should strive to learn, before they die, what they are running from and to and why," said James Thurber. If Don is beginning to step off the escape path and take a serious look at his inner life, then we can rejoice. This is what we want to see in him. In the chapter ahead, we'll see if Don can move a step further—into deepening surrender to the Holy Spirit.

STORY FROM THE MISSION FIELD

TODD MENKE

I started wearing my green rubber bracelet in early 2009. I had just had the opportunity to lead a group of men, from my church, through a Men's Fraternity™ 16-week program on *Winning at Work & Home*. After the program concluded, I decided to purchase for each man a green rubber bracelet with a message that was the central theme of the course. On one side of the bracelet were the words SECRET OF LIFE. On the opposite side was DIE TO SELF. When my oldest daughter, Grace, who was eight years old at the time, first saw my bracelet, she was confused and scared that it might mean my actual death. Little did she know (or could possibly understand) that the message was actually a life-giving message that started with her adoption in 2002.

216

You see my wife, Kellie and I had struggled for years with starting a family and after lots of prayers and difficult times, we decided to adopt a little girl from China. Kellie was and continues to be a spiritual person with an amazing faith that still inspires me to this day. Although I would like to tell you I was fully prepared to give God all the credit for our decision to adopt, I was actually nowhere near to being a spiritually mature man. The truth is that the decision for "me" was self-centered on my desire to start a family with my wife. God was on the periphery I suppose, but I was still consumed with what "I wanted". I was living a *self-life*. All of that began to change that day in Hunan, China, when I held my daughter in my arms for the first time.

For a lot of parents, naturally, that feeling is all too familiar, but, you see, that experience set me on a course of discovery to find out more about God and what He wanted me to be. For the first time, it was not *all about me*. This little girl was now dependent on my wife and me—her mom and dad!—to care for her in ways I could not possibly comprehend. My path to *die to self* was further influenced by the adoption of our son, Edward, in 2003, from South Korea and our second daughter, Amelia, in 2005, again from Hunan, China. When I began to put my children ahead of myself, I saw a pattern that led me to look at worldly things differently.

When the recession hit in 2008, my business began to suffer. I thought I had everything, but I soon discovered I possessed nothing. Everything that was important "of this world" seemed to disappear. Yet instead of weakening my faith, my discovery process actually led me to a stronger faith and a better understanding of what God wanted me to be. He had me in His sights, but I can't say I ever realized I was a target. He wanted me to *die to self*, but looking back now, this was a two-stage process for me.

In the first stage, I was led to start living in this world as Jesus lived, putting others in front of myself. This new approach to my "external" life positively affected my marriage, my relationship with my children and my relationship with friends and others I came into contact with. The second stage was the ultimate reward, though. As He began to change my heart and show me how a *die-to-self* approach would change my "inner" life, I realized He lived in me and was part of every facet of my life.

I had been living a compartmentalized life and God resided in one of those compartments. In order to change this, He showed me His plan through **Scripture, prayers and quiet time with Him alone**; my divided heart was fused together. He actually showed me what a full heart looked like and I realized it was impossible to keep Him out of the other compartments of my life. He was meant to live inside me and be a part of every facet of my life, but I literally had to be willing to tune Him in so I could listen and understand how to follow His will. That spiritual connection requires serious effort and just like any muscle, my mind and heart needed training and attention to maintain a good strong reception. The good news is that it can be done; you just have to make the choice to *die to self* and He will take you there!

Your Next-Step Action Plan

FOR YOUR JOURNEY INWARD: PERSONAL SPIRITUAL RETREAT*

Set aside a day with God to spend precisely six hours following these instructions exactly.

Go somewhere: Make it a place where you can be completely alone—outdoors, if possible (the seashore, the country, the mountains, the park). It should be somewhere you will not see anyone (at least to speak to). The only person you want to speak to and hear from is God.

You will need: A journal, two pens, drink, snack, beach-type chair and comfortable clothes.

First two hours: Begin with prayer. Then just relax and let your mind wander aimlessly as you stroll about, sit, lie on your back and watch the clouds drift across the sky. *This is tough, but hang in there.*

Second two hours: Let your mind go back to your earliest recollection of childhood and, very slowly during these two hours, think about the events of your life through the years, as you bring yourself up to the present.

As you think about these events, think of the **GOOD** these things have brought into your life, the positive side: even tragedy builds character.

Look at the good side of everything you think about. Most important, consider and answer this question: *Where has God been present throughout my life?* Record these valuable insights.

Third two hours: Think about the present, where you are in your life now, today. Think about yourself, your family, friends and business associates. Realize how much there is to be thankful for and to enjoy. *What is really important to you?*

Prioritize your life and goals as follows: **Spiritual, Family, Personal, Work.**

What new capability do you want to take on? (Learn to play the guitar? Fish? Golf?). Pray about what God really wants to accomplish through you over the next year and how He is leading you to achieve it by going after it, not in a hectic fashion, but in a determined manner; move steadily toward it.

God has an awesome adventure awaiting you over the next year, as you have just spent six hours hearing about!

Review your goals the first day of each month. In 12 months, repeat the above steps.

It has been to my great benefit to have set aside six hours for a personal spiritual retreat* annually since 1985. I have notebooks filled with vision, goals, desires and outcomes! What a delight to see God's will in any life communicated over and over again, all because I took time to seriously understand where He wanted me to invest my life.

*Developed by Executive Development Systems.

For Personal Reflection

1. To what degree do I feel myself to be "the object of God's delight"? Why?

2. As I compare and contrast my life experience and attitudes with Don's, my thoughts are. . .

3. Can I relate to Gary's struggle with sexual temptation? How do I typically deal with this struggle or some other temptation I struggle with?

4. What would it mean for me to "step off the escape path" and take a serious look at my inner life? What first step could I take?

For Group Discussion

1. Talk about what it means to each of you to know that you are beloved by God. What makes it easy or hard to remember this as you go through life?

2. What does it mean to you, personally, to "grow in openheartedness"? Do you believe this is an important journey for men? Explain your response to the group.

3. Share: For me, the biggest *challenge* of the "inward journey" is _____. The greatest *blessing* of it is_____.

4. Discuss the statement by Carl Jung: "Neurosis is an escape from legitimate suffering." What does this mean and how does it apply to you or men you know?

5. Talk about the concept of masculine spirituality being so related to bodily desire. What can this teach us about relating to men in our ministries?

Chapter 13

Blessed in His Journey Godward: Surrender

I have been reflecting on the inestimable value of "broken things". Broken pitchers gave ample light for victory (Judges 7:19-21); broken bread was more than enough for all the hungry (Matthew 14:19-21); a broken box gave fragrance to all the world (Mark 14:3, 9); and a broken body is salvation to all who believe and receive the Saviour (I Corinthians 11:24). And what cannot the Broken One do with our broken plans, projects, and hearts?

V. Raymond Edmund[1]

If "home" is the image that speaks of openheartedness to the true self, which is a key to the first masculine journey, then let me suggest *wine and water* as a biblical image for the second journey. It gives us a way to visualize something important about loving and surrendering to God.

Don, you keep talking about feeling a "loss of control" in your life, but almost as if it's a good thing? What's with that?

"On one hand, I feel like I can't really make good decisions. I look back over 'Don's life' so far—my teen years and 20s and 30s—and I see a lot of messed up situations and hurt people lying in my wake. It's like I'm a bulldozer, going down the road of life just running over people.

"On the other hand, the thing about getting back into church is that at some point you have to kneel down. That's the part that is making an impact on me now. I don't hear much of the words; it's the kneeling that means something. . . and then holding out my hands for the cup of wine. It's like all I can do is 'receive' at this point, you know? I've got nothing to give."

He's Deepening in Surrender

An Episcopal priest once shared with me some of the "secret prayers" he says during the celebration of the Eucharist. For example, as he pours a bit of water into the wine, he says, "By the mystery of this water and wine, may we come to share in the divinity of Christ, as He humbled Himself to share in our humanity." This whispered prayer echoes the powerful proclamation of the apostle Peter, that we "might be partakers of the divine nature" (see 2 Peter 1:4). I'm told that underneath the English text for the word "partakers" is the Greek word *koinonia*, commonly trans-lated *fellowship*, *sharing*, or *communion*.

Wine, for the Christian worshiper, goes back to the upper room and the last supper of Jesus with His disciples. He was going to His death and on the cross His blood, mingled with water, flowed out for the sins of the world. As the co-min-gling of water with wine was a common practice in Jesus's day, no doubt Jesus did something similar to our present-day practice at the church's altar: mixing water with the wine before He gave the cup to the disciples.

What does it mean? Surely it symbolizes a profound truth of our relationship to God: it is to be a growth in *union* with Him—mixing, co-mingling. In the incarnation, Jesus took up into Himself our humanity, perfecting it with His sinlessness and ascending to heaven with it as the Author and Perfector of our faith. In a marvelous exchange, we also partake in His nature. It's not that we become God ourselves, but we do receive the privilege of being the tabernacles in which He dwells. By infusing His life into us, He transforms us. Jesus prayed for all future believers when He asked,

> . . .*that they all may be one; as thou, Father, art in me, and I in thee, that they also may be one in us: that the world may believe that thou hast sent me.* (John 17:21)

Just as Jesus is one person with two natures—fully God, fully man—we can see ourselves similarly as one person with the old nature and the new nature competing for dominance, moment by moment. That new nature (see Colossians 3:10; Ephesians 4:24) is actually the presence of God in us by His indwelling Spirit. As we surrender to His influence, we strengthen the union between us. Through this partaking of divinity inside, our new nature (which looks like Jesus!) becomes more and more evident on the outside.

Let's look a little more closely at all of this from a strictly biblical point of view. One of the things to know about the infant-baptized Don is that he is saved. More specifically, he has *been* saved, is *being* saved and he *shall be* saved. The Bible speaks often of this salvation under three great theological terms: justification, sanctification and glorification.

SALVATION in three biblical stages. . .

Justification: Position - I have *been* saved from the Penalty of Sin by God's eternal *declaration*.

Sanctification: Process - I am *being* saved from the Power of Sin by my daily *decisions*.

Glorification: Pinnacle - I *shall be* saved from the Presence of Sin in my heavenly *dwelling*.

Explanation:

- *Justification* is the declaration of God's "not guilty" verdict upon us, based on the payment of sin's penalty through the atoning cross of the Lamb of God. It places us in the **position** of full acceptance with the Father; we're declared forgiven, adopted, redeemed and righteous in His sight.
  Key Scriptures: Romans 4 and 5; 1 Corinthians 6:11; Galatians 2:16.

- *Sanctification* is the **process** of our daily growth in holiness. We gradually "become what we are"—that is, we become in practice what God has declared us to be: righteous. In a daily walk with God, yielding to the Holy Spirit, we are enabled by grace to avoid sin and actively serve in the kingdom. Sanctifying grace continually cleanses us, helping us take on the character of Christ and His virtues, producing the fruits of the Spirit and exercising our spiritual gifts.
  Key Scriptures: Romans 7 and 8; 1 Corinthians 1, 6, 7; 1 Thessalonians 4; 2 Thessalonians 2:13; Titus 2:5, 6.

- *Glorification* is the **pinnacle**, or culmination, of salvation in which we finally arrive in God's presence and remain with Him forever. God has declared us righteous, worked within us to produce practical holiness and finally has brought to pass what He intended: we are like Jesus. Even our bodies have become new and sin and temptation are no longer issues for us. We receive the privilege of "reigning with Christ" throughout eternity.

Key Scriptures: Romans 8:17-30.

I stress these stages for good reason. Knowing them can clear up a lot of confusion about the respective role of "works" and "grace" in a man's Christian growth. We work for God, in the process of sanctification, out of our gratitude for the gift of justification—not in order to earn our standing with God, but to show our thankfulness for already receiving it. In other words, Christ took up His cross for us to make us His own; now He calls us to take up our cross for Him with thankful hearts. Justification is the beginning of the process of salvation, the end being sanctification, the perfection of our souls, without which we could never "see" God. Grace is operative and essential throughout that process, but so is our response.

MIKE FORBES

(Continued from Chapter 3)

GOD IS LOVE

From those days in late 2005, I started to think more about the existence of GOD. I began to look around and experiment with what I might and might not be willing to believe. It was at this time I was warned about "spiritual warfare". GDO was not going to go down without a fight. And sure enough, literally within days, I was swept into an obsessive relationship with another woman. What was I thinking?

It was crazy! The harder I tried to get out and get away, the more I was reeled in like a fish on a hook. It seemed everyone from "my old life" was resurfacing and rooting for the death of my marriage.

Christmas 2005 came. For all I knew, it was the last time our family would sit together for dinner, even if it was at some impersonal restaurant. It was a surreal, hopeless feeling. It was not what I wanted, not what my wife wanted and definitely not on our children's Christmas list. Yet, it seemed inevitable.

Several more weeks of denial, anger, fear and warfare followed. I just could not accept what I now call the "biggie" (see Romans 10:9) until one day in February. I had stooped to new lows in my personal actions that I just could not accept in myself. I had nothing left of my pride, my integrity, my self-worth. I had nowhere else to go. It was at that moment that Christ came to me. I fell to my knees, a broken man and asked that Christ would enter into my heart.

It was so important at that time to have strong Christ-centered men move into action. I was challenged to read parts of Scripture during the week and meet for lunch to discuss the concepts. I was also immediately invited to join an accountability group with four other Christian men at various stages in their walk. I was engaged immediately.

This began my climb back out of the hole I had dug for myself. Even though Christ had started healing me, reconciliation with my family would take time, a lot of patience and most important, forgiveness. Over a period of several months, we were able to patch our lives back together only with the help of Jesus and my brothers in Christ.

I consider my story a miracle God executed to show men that there is a way out of the cycle of self-centered indulgence and excess. One crucial aspect of this miracle was the presence of other strong, spiritual men God used to walk the man in crisis "off the cliff" with love and respect.

As my faith in the Lord has grown through the years, I also have been fortunate to work with other men who have found themselves in the same condition in which I had been. From sharing Christ's love, to leading accountability groups, to leading men's church organizations, nothing would have happened if there were not strong Christian men leading the charge with integrity and sincerity in my life.

It's a Formation Process

So our goal for Don is that he take up this journey of surrender to the process of sanctification, day by day. It's what I call the secret of life: living in union with God, through Jesus Christ, in the power of the Holy Spirit.

> *You said, Don, that things were starting to happen in your life that you could only explain as "spiritual". Can you tell me more about that?*
> "I think it started when one of the guys at St. Luke's mentioned a prayer that seemed to turn him onto a new path in life. I wrote it down and later I tried it—prayed it a lot of times over a few days. It goes like this: 'God, as much as I know of myself, I give to as much as I know of You.' I was impressed with that prayer because it was so simple, yet it seemed to say everything I wanted to tell God. I just wanted to kind of give up on the whole idea of making my life—and all its mess—into something else. If there

is a God, I thought maybe He'd have to be the one to change me.

"Anyway, praying that prayer changed my direction, too. I can see that now, when I look back."

Don's case is uniquely his. But the process is pretty standard for all of us. It is simply surrendering to the workings of Christian formation, for *Christian formation* is *Christ formed* in us. As Paul wrote to the churches:

> *My little children, for whom I labor in birth again until Christ is formed in you. . .* (Galatians 4:19)
> *For whom He foreknew, He also predestined to be conformed to the image of His Son, that He might be the firstborn among many brethren.* (Romans 8:29)

For Don, it will start looking like this.

- *More and more, he keeps Christ on the throne of his life.* If we imagine the inner life as a heart with a kingly throne at its center, we see Don bowing before that throne. Christ is sitting there. In practical terms, this means that his decision making is improving. He is consulting his Lord. He's looking to the example of Christ and seeking to follow in His steps as he goes through the day. The other men in the church are helping him stay on this path. Though past decisions may have landed him in plenty of distressing and tangled messes, Don is teachable and willing to start untangling it all.
- *More and more, he is filled with the Holy Spirit.* "Be not drunk with wine," said Paul in Ephesians 5:18, "but be filled with the Spirit." Realize that the Holy Spirit is a person, not a force or other entity, so we can't get more of Him. In this case, "filled"

means "controlled by" or "yielded to". So, *the Holy Spirit can get more of us* as we yield to His gentle influence. If Don is learning to do this, he will begin to display the fruits of holy character. Many "lists" appear in the Bible telling us what that looks like, but here are just three.

Galatians 5:22, 23—love, joy, peace, long-suffering, gentleness, goodness, faith, meekness, temperance—the traditional fruits of the Spirit

1 Corinthians 13:13—faith, hope, love—the traditional theological virtues

1 Peter 1:5-8—faith, moral excellence, knowledge, self-control, endurance, godliness, brotherly affection, love for everyone

Yielding to the Holy Spirit is the daily aspect of the surrender we've been exploring. Our job as leaders is to encourage this in every man we work with. In a sense, it is helping Don in his growth to stop living in Romans 7 and begin living in Romans 8.

> *For what I am doing, I do not understand. For what I will to do, that I do not practice; but what I hate, that I do... What a wretched man I am!* (Romans 7:15, 24)
> *But you are not in the flesh but in the Spirit, if indeed the Spirit of God dwells in you. Now if anyone does not have the Spirit of Christ, he is not His.* (Romans 8:9)

C. S. Lewis, in *Mere Christianity,* used some marvelous images for describing what is happening to us on this path of surrender. He likened it to a "good infection" that spreads within a body. It's the infection of real life from God, changing our natural life into a spiritual life. This is the Holy

Spirit taking over in each area of our lives that we open to him. Lewis also said that it is like having a toy tin soldier on the shelf: it has been inert, lifeless, but the tin is gradually turning into flesh. That toy soldier is "obstinate" though, because the natural life has to die.

> **Because the whole difficulty for us is that the natural life has to be, in a sense, "killed", Jesus chose an earthly career which involved the killing of His human desires at every turn—poverty, misunderstanding from His own family, betrayal by one of His intimate friends, being jeered at and manhandled by the police, and execution by torture. And then, after being thus killed—killed every day in a sense—the human creature in Him, because it was united to the divine Son, came to life again. The Man in Christ rose again: not only the God. That is the whole point. For the first time we saw a real man. One tin soldier—real tin, just like the rest—had come fully and splendidly alive. . . .One of our own race has this new life: if we get close to Him we shall catch it from Him.[2]**

- *More and more, he practices recollection.* One of the significant roles of the local church leadership with Don is to help him keep remembering. We have said he is beloved by God and we have encouraged that sense of identity. But a big challenge in spiritual growth is our tendency to keep forgetting who we are. We forget that divine life has infused our souls and bodies. We are called to come back to reality, over and over again, until our entire self-image is renewed.

One leader of men, Joe Glenn Smith of Valdosta, Georgia,[3] hammers on the scriptural concept of "in Christ" with the men he has mentored. These two words appear together about ninety times in the New Testament and they are powerful. The Christian man, in all his "walking around" through his days, actually goes "in Christ". Joe says to think of a pet shop. If you go there to look at the hamsters, you will likely see at least one of those little critters moving around inside a clear plastic ball. When he walks, he makes the ball move. Everywhere that animal travels, he is "in ball". Everything he meets, meets the ball first. Everything he bumps into bumps into the ball.

It is like that with us. We are "in Christ". Every person we meet bumps into Jesus. Everywhere we go, we are encased in His life and shining forth His character. Every bit of reality that we enter into, we have taken Jesus there. Conversely, everything that Jesus has done is ours by union with Him—His death to sin, His resurrection to new life, His fellowship with the Father and so on. That is our reality, our identity. Can we remember it?

A growing Don, being nurtured in the formation processes of your local church, has a stunning portrait: we see him sheathed in Christ and remembering this as his identity, more and more.

What helps Don *remember*? Consider this.

> *Your image of yourself is changing, right? Is that how you'd describe it?*
> "Right. I keep getting reminded that I'm a Christian, that I'm not alone. The thing that keeps bringing me back to it is being with other Christian guys. I know I can't be at church all the time, but coming to group on Friday mornings helps a lot.
> "The other thing that really 'set the hook' on knowing I'm a Christian was the men's retreat. We

had a lot of activity, but for me the quiet times were so amazing. I mean, think about it: when does anybody ever get time alone, just me and myself, with no extra 'noise'? We had to turn off our cell phones and just be alone. That taught me that I can remember who I really am—a follower of Jesus—wherever I am and whenever I want. I just have to change the channel in my mind and determine to be still inside. That's what I've started trying to do, especially at work, where it's so hectic. There have been times when I've really needed to remember who I am—rather than blowing up at somebody or getting hacked off about a situation."

Again, what helps Don with building recollection into his life? That is the crucial part where you, the leader of men, come in. In the ongoing discipling process, you encourage him to remember by. . .

. . .helping him gain the habit of daily **Bible reading**. There is no substitute for this. A man growing in Christ, the living Word, is consuming (and being consumed by!) the written Word.

. . .showing him how to **pray**. Don can recollect who he really is through "constant contact" with the one in whom he dwells and who dwells in him. Remember that a Christian is being infused with divine life. Prayer is paying attention to that life, whether in words or in silence. It is attending to the holy, either way.

. . .inviting him into **fellowship** and accountability. We "set the hook" in this process by encouraging Don to mark the highs and lows of his spiritual journey through interacting about it with other men. We all need social interaction and a good men's ministry will provide that—times just for fun and being together. But fellowship is different. Fellowship is being with one another as *we relate around the things of the spiritual life*. As Don is doing that, he's remembering who he is in Christ.

Recollection is just another way of saying what the apostle Paul called us all to do: "pray without ceasing" (1 Thessalonians 5:17). It's how we become increasingly grounded in the truth of God's never-ending presence with us, no matter our life situation. As the great devotional writer Oswald Chambers said in *My Utmost for His Highest,* "Having the reality of God's presence is not dependent on our being in a particular circumstance or place, but is only dependent on our determination to keep the Lord before us continually."[4]

- *More and more, he experiences gratitude and joy.* Christian formation and growth is like a spiral. We navigate through our trials and tests of faith. We experience relief and consolation with our successes. Then comes the next trial and we seem to repeat the test, but at a new level, with new contours, different people, and changed circumstances. And as we emerge, significantly matured, we rejoice—and then comes the next test of faith.

In this way God builds us up and creates ever-stronger muscles of faith for us so that we can enter more demanding and satisfying projects in His name. All of this works a deep joy into our lives. Even amidst times of great sorrow, when we could hardly say we are happy, a spiritual joy still reverberates in us.

Someone has said that the prime quality of the Christian life is a sense of gratitude. I am coming to believe that. Looking back over the years, I see God's hand at work in me, guiding and sustaining, carrying me through. Every

Christian man who is growing in Christ can attest to that kind of joy and give grateful thanks. If we see that kind of attitude blossoming in Don, that is a sign of our success in working with him through the church. Next, he'll want to get involved with a group of men who can help him belong and serve. That's the chapter ahead.

Your Next-Step Action Plan

READY TO ANSWER? Be sure you have a handle on the basic theology of salvation. Review the chart and think through how it applies to your personal "story" of becoming and being a Christian.

Then suppose someone were to ask you, "How can I become a Christian?" Think about what you would like to say about this! In fact, you might wish to develop an "elevator talk" for yourself that is always ready.

> *Let your speech always be with grace, seasoned with salt, that you may know how you ought to answer each one.* (Colossians 4:6)

The elevator talk is a two-minute presentation of the gospel that is clear and compelling and that speaks of your own experience, as well. Try writing one out! Who knows? Next time you step onto an elevator, someone might say to you, "I see you're reading a book about church. Now, how could that be interesting?" Two minutes. . . *go!*

For Personal Reflection

1. When have I felt myself to be a "broken thing"? How was that good or bad? What did it do to my relationship with God?

2. How would I describe my level of surrender to God these days?

3. What things tend to deepen my surrender—or hold me back?

4. Where am I with Bible reading, prayer and fellowship at this moment?

5. Sit for a while in God's presence, in silence and notice any joy that arises. Spend some time in thanks to God.

For Group Discussion

1. Talk about what it means for each of you to "journey in surrender".

2. In your opinion, how would the typical guy you know respond to this chapter's theme?

3. Seriously study the chart on salvation in this chapter. Talk about any way this helps clarify the theology for you. What does it say, for example, about the relationship of faith to works?

4. What is the meaning and impact of C. S. Lewis's "tin soldier" quote for you?

Chapter 14

Blessed in His Journey Outward: Belonging and Service

An African Christian once said to me: "You Americans think of Christianity as a farm with a fence. Your question is 'Are you inside the fence or outside of it?' We Africans think differently. We think of Christianity as a farm with no fence. Our question is, 'Are you heading towards the farm, or away from it?'"

The church's identity is not defined primarily by its edges, but by its center: when we're focused on Christ, the sole source of our identity, no intruder poses a threat. No alien hops a fence, because there is no fence. Boundaries are determined by proximity to the Holy Spirit's [attraction], not by arbitrary human borders. . . .The more churches lose our ability to barricade ourselves off from one another, the more God's grace flows through us into the world.

-Kendra Creasy Dean[1]

In December 1984, I began to feel a leading in my life to become, as I put it at the time, "more spiritually involved." But I really didn't know how to live in union with God. I had done little of the journeying we've been exploring in these chapters: the journey into self, God and others. My wife Laura and I were involved in our Methodist church in Atlanta, but I needed to focus.

My turnaround began with a New Year's resolution. I knew our church had a weekly men's prayer breakfast and I told Laura, "That's what I want to do—get involved with a group of Christian men. . . .I promise to do it. . . faithfully." The little smile that crept up into her face told me this was a good decision.

I went to that first meeting, at six in the morning, with fear and trepidation. *Would I be asked to "share a little about myself," tell my life's story, or just start right out with confessing my most embarrassing sins?*

It was a simple format—some informal talking and eating, some Bible study—and the pastor, Bill Floyd, was always there with us. At the end of a study time, they did something I thought very strange. They stood, held hands and prayed. At that point, I thought, *Yuk!* I also thought, *Where's the nearest exit?*

I stayed for the next three years. Every single week I was there and these men guided me. I learned through them what an openhearted approach to life could be. I learned what living in union with God through Jesus Christ was all about—and I started living it. I took small steps forward, but with constant encouragement. Best of all, I harbored a growing sense of being in the right place: "I really *belong* to these guys!"

Now remember that ministry to men is about being **called**, being **mentored**, being **equipped** and being **sent**—through the church. In other words, what we want men to find in our local congregations is that they are involved in the great adventure of transforming the world. It's where their longing has always been, but it's an adventure we enjoy *together*.

He's Connecting

I had asked Don several questions in our time together. One of them was: *What do younger men need from the church today?* Part of his response went like this.

> **Developing fellowship with other male members of the church is becoming important. The Men's Conference I attended at our denominational camp last year was helpful. I'm not naturally good at sharing my feelings, a combination of Southern, male and shyness. But it helped hearing that not only were others going through what I was, but some had gone through and come out the other side.**
>
> **I also wanted to let you know that I spoke with my pastor last week and have dates set for church membership and confirmation. I do feel the talks we've had and the general support you're giving me were very instrumental in my making the decision to move forward on those two and I wanted to thank you.**

Don is on the third part of the journey, the "neighbor" part of Christ's command. For our purposes, *neighbor* is the other guy in the church—the one who needs me and the one who can go with me in the adventure of carrying out the Great Commission. Together we will win others into the kingdom and teach them how to be Christ-followers.

I know of hundreds of men, from every background and denomination, who meet together to share their joys and sorrows, their life concerns and prayer concerns, their spiritual insights and questions—in short, to share their lives with one another. Groups usually meet at lunchtime or during an early morning breakfast. Or they may meet in a home during the evening.

According to a study done by Promise Keepers, our society views men as mostly self-reliant, unable to feel or express emotion, unconcerned about fellowship, using people, but loving things, primarily competitive and too macho. If this is the case, then seeing Don "wanting to belong" is a step toward improving that situation.

What Draws the Unchurched Guy?

In an article in *New Man Magazine* titled "The Battle for the Hearts of Men", George Barna cites seven things that unchurched men said would draw them to the church.[2] Here's a summary.

1. **A credible offer of meaning and purpose in life**
2. **Practical and applicable help in self-understanding**
3. **Solutions to the problems and challenges of their everyday lives**
4. **A clear and reasonable approach to understanding who God is and how He is important in daily life**
5. **Men's ministry that touches them where they are**
6. **An offer of practical help with family and child rearing concerns**
7. **A way to find friendships that are trustworthy and offer potential for lifelong bonds**

Many men in our churches actually long for a group in which they can safely reveal their problems and receive the support they need to overcome them. Finding and

befriending a fellow struggler brings tremendous encouragement, as men discover they are not alone in their destructive
relational patterns or "secret sins". I can't emphasize enough
the importance of this kind of fellowship, which is based on
serious self-learning and candid sharing.

What happens when men do *not* find a group where
this kind of sharing takes place? They'll often bog down
in their spiritual journeys in one of two ways. First, some
men *continue seeking to control their circumstances.* This
stance characterizes the man who says, "I believe I *should* be
joyful; I *should* feel fulfilled. But I never seem to reach it. I
try and try, but something always goes wrong." When faced
with dissatisfaction in life, we may seek to overcome it by
trying to force our happiness. It never works.

Second, some men *keep trying to "act the part".* This is
almost the opposite approach. These are the guys who try to
act as though things really are working out great all the time.
Not content to savor the blessings and joys God sprinkles
into their years, they may pretend unbroken daily bliss. In
effect, they begin to fake the Christian life, wearing the mask
of continual victory. And, of course, that doesn't work for
long either.

The third and more truly Christian approach to life, as
we've seen, is left to those guys who are *learning to embrace
the pain*—the pain and the struggle of spiritual pilgrimage.
It's not the easy route to take, but it is the most honest. It
brings us down to a basic reality, that everything we are and
have is a product of the pure, unconditional grace of our
heavenly Father. And here's the key point: this approach to
Christian living *cannot be done in a vacuum.* It requires fellowship, mutual encouragement and ongoing accountability,
as men meet together to discuss their progress (successes
and failures) along with their prayer concerns. That is the
way they help each other live for God, all along the way to
Christian maturity.[3]

Of course, meeting together involves a lot of fun and laughter, too! It should surprise no one that joking and good-natured ribbing fills a great deal of the time together. But I would like to take us back, once again, to the area of sexual temptation. In talking with men over the years, I've found that this one area is a constant source of potential stumbling. Many bear the scars of wounded warriors in this arena. Even among the leaders of the church, the casualty list is devastating. Who of us couldn't name any number of former prominent pastors who have succumbed to moral failings? But why?

Henri Nouwen, in his book for church leaders, *In the Name of Jesus,* ties the phenomenon specifically to the lack of close fellowship among men, especially among mature Christian leaders.

> **It is precisely the men and women who are dedicated to spiritual leadership who are easily subject to very raw carnality. The reason for this is that they do not know how to live the truth of the Incarnation. They separate themselves from their own concrete community, try to deal with their needs by ignoring them or satisfying them in distant or anonymous places, and then experience an increasing split between their own most private inner world and the good news they announce. When spirituality becomes spiritualization, life in the body becomes carnality.[4]**

One of our great goals for Don is to keep his spirituality from becoming a spiritualization. If he is "out of touch" with his real self or with the Lord who dwells in him, this can happen. But when he is out of touch with his brothers in Christ, spiritualization will most assuredly happen and it becomes a potentially fatal alienation.

Jesus had a powerful ministry management style that counteracted this deadly danger. He called, mentored and equipped 12 men and poured His life into them. Then He gave them a compelling vision (Matthew 28:19, 20) and sent them out for adventure. The result was disciple makers building His church. **However, He did not send them to do the work alone.**

> *And He called the twelve to Himself, and began to send them out two by two, and gave them power over unclean spirits.*(Mark 6:7)
>
> *After these things the Lord appointed seventy others also, and sent them two by two before His face into every city and place where He Himself was about to go.* (Luke 10:1)

So, What Does He Look Like?

I asked you to look at a portrait of Don as if he were experiencing an intentional process of Christian formation for men through your church. We considered what he would "look like" and we assumed this would give us a sense of our goals with him as men's ministry leaders.

We've seen that the growing-in-Christ Don is on a spiritual journey that takes him in-ward, God-ward and out-ward. That is, he'll be developing an openhearted stance toward his inner life, growing in surrender to the indwelling Holy Spirit and gaining a sense of belonging to his neighbors—particularly, the men on a kingdom-mission with him in the church. As a leader, seeing the picture of Don taking these initial steps greatly encourages me. In fact, seeing such sights is exactly why I am in this ministry.

STORY FROM THE MISSION FIELD

JEFF KERN

My spiritual awakening started in the fall of 1985 right after the birth of our first child, Maggie. This phase, I could call equipping, sprung into action when my wife, Debbie and I attended Cursillo, a weekend-long, Christian leadership retreat. It was as if a light bulb turned up to 1,000 watts, which led us both to become more spiritually focused with the ongoing support of our sponsors/mentors. Our sponsors brought us to a weekly accountability group, where we shared our Christian lives. We became inspired to volunteer on leadership teams for future Cursillo weekends, which strengthened our faith, weekend by weekend.

This led to another *big* step in my faith development, as I stepped into a prison ministry called Kairos. I grew up in a small Ohio town that had a federal penitentiary and I frequently played youth baseball and football exhibition games inside the prison for the inmates and grew very comfortable in that setting and service. A Kairos team consists of about 25 spiritually mature men who carefully prepare for many weeks to share their lives with inmates on a weekend-long Christian retreat. I was blessed to have actually helped lead several inmates to know the Lord by allowing the Holy Spirit to lead me in ways I never could have imagined.

We met Jay and Laura Crouse at Church of the Redeemer in the early 1990s. Shortly thereafter, we shared a Cursillo weekend, during which we connected instantly. I was fortunate to be part of Jay's early development of men's ministry at Redeemer and the surrounding southwest Florida area. One of the most meaningful programs Jay has introduced is "Raising a Modern-day Knight" This is a program for a father and son to grow closer through a series of bonding events and provides the child with Christian tools and mentors before the son goes off on his own. We have both been involved in our own sons' rites of passage programs and share the passion of encouraging other fathers to be involved in this important ritual.

Then Jay rolled out one of his most successful endeavors, "Equipping the 70", an ecumenical training for Christian men to go out into the world to evangelize, much as Jesus did with His 12 disciples, two-by-two. This term *two-by-two* made me very uncomfortable, hesitant and downright fearful. We have all experienced it: the knock on the door, two young men in white shirts and ties, waiting for you to open the door to shove you "the pamphlet" so they can show you the way! I had a similar, uneasy feeling when going through the equipping phase. I had some figuring out to do and time would reveal the answer. The Lord did not need or want me to be uncomfortable when I share my faith with others. My close relationship with the Lord is the key; then He uses my 30-plus years of spiritual experiences and He finds the right person for me to witness to or just be friends with. I don't need to go door to door or stand on street corners; He sends those He chooses into my path and oftentimes into the path of two of us.

What I didn't grasp is that Jay and I had actually been practicing the two-by-two approach all along. The very act of men's ministry is two by two. God puts men in need into our paths; we listen, encourage and support them. I have many people in my life who are my two-by-two partners. Debbie, my wife of 31 years, is my number one two-by-two partner. I don't think our children would have gone to church if we were not firm on attending together with them. We have brought many couples to our church home over the years and always two by two. My rector, Father Fred Robinson and I are also two-by-two partners. Even though he may never have thought of it that way, he asks me to talk to a new couple attending church or to bring a struggling husband to our weekly accountability group.

It all starts with our biggest strength and ally, the true number one partner in the two-by-two journey, Jesus. He calls us, mentors and equips us, then sends us out to share His love in our everyday life and spiritual walk.

Your Next-Step Action Plan

MEN'S MINISTRY IS DAUNTING. As you finish this book, think again about what a challenge it is to start and maintain a men's ministry in your mainline denominational church. The obstacles are real and daunting, and the risk of failure is great. But never become discouraged! Trust God with your life and the lives of the men you seek to reach.

Ask yourself:

1. Read and meditate upon the words in 2 Corinthians 4:6-11. What does this Scripture passage say about the faith and courage of the apostle?

2. What does it say about your attitude regarding the future of men in the church—and in your local congregation?

3. What is God calling you to do now?

For Personal Reflection

1. 1. When have I seen "connection" in action in me? In another guy? How does this happen?

2. Am I in a group of men that meets regularly for fellowship? If not, could I start a group?

3. What does the statement by Henri Nouwen cited in this chapter say to me about the dangers that come with spiritual leadership? How do I protect myself?

4. Analyze the "picture" of Don at the end of this chapter. Think about how that picture inspires you and your ministry. Ask God to use you as a soldier in advancing his kingdom through discipling men like Don.

5. Do a personal Bible study on this passage from the apostle Paul.

    For it is the God who commanded light to shine out of darkness, who has shone in our hearts to give the light of the knowledge of the glory of God in the face of Jesus Christ.

    But we have this treasure in earthen vessels, that the excellence of the power may be of God and not of us.

    We are hard-pressed on every side, yet not crushed; we are perplexed, but not in despair; persecuted, but not forsaken; struck down, but not destroyed—always carrying about in the body the dying of the Lord Jesus, that the life of Jesus also may be manifested in our body.

*For we who live are always delivered to death
for Jesus's sake, that the life of Jesus also may be
manifested in our mortal flesh.* (2 Corinthians 4:6-11)

For Group Discussion

1. What is your response to the opening quotation in this
   chapter—the contrasting of African and American
   perspectives on the church?

2. Talk through the chart titled, "What Draws the
   Unchurched Guy". Come up with a list of specific
   applications to your own church's men's ministry.

3. Why is close fellowship so important? Why is it
   "scary" for many men? What helps break down
   barriers among men so that healthy fellowship
   can deepen?

4. What problems develop for men when they become
   isolated? What have you observed or experienced
   with this?

Epilogue

Thank you for taking this big, holy audacious journey with me: men and the church—is there a future?

Our journey began with a rather poignant view of the mainline denominational churches communicating a message of benign neglect toward not only the men in the pews of their local churches, but to the unchurched, lost men in our communities. And although this church attitude has not been done meanly, nor intentionally or even in our subconscious, the readily available data on the dramatic, decades long decline in church membership, especially by men, points to at least benign neglect being a contributing factor in this decline.

With this landscape and a conviction that leaders and emerging leaders are called to take legitimate responsibility for improving the situation, I then set a course to show through examples from local churches and personal stories what can transpire in the life of the church when benign neglect goes and in its place an intentional Christian formation process for men is implemented.

We investigated broadly and deeply who the unchurched man is today, strategies to welcome men back to the local, denominational church and then provided a compelling vision of the churched man and the inspired results.

Leaders and emerging leaders, your calling is to build God's kingdom. I have chosen to do this man-to-man. If your hearts and minds have been quickened by what you have read throughout these pages, I challenge you to take the right next step: borrow every resource, idea, insight raised up in this book, expand on all of this, leverage it, be creative and intentional and join hundreds of church leaders and emerging leaders committed to capturing the hearts of men. The future of the local church depends on your next step.

As for me, on May 24, 2013, I celebrated 25 years of ministry focus on men and the church. What a breathtaking season of ministry. At a wonderful celebration breakfast on May 24, I announced my retirement from ministry—at the 50th celebration of ministry to men in 2038. I look forward to working with you in the mission field during these next 25years.

Celebrating 25 years of men's ministry: Jud Boedecker, Jeff Kern, Jay Crouse and Tramm Hudson with the famous Klondike bars.

Acknowledgments

In exploring the Crouse family genealogy, I found ministry pursuits have been a core passion for generations. So, I stand on the shoulders of my family members, including my mother and father, to whom I owe a great debt of gratitude for their Christian conviction and faith.

Let me continue my acknowledgments where most acknowledgments seem to end: my family. My wife, Laura, has been a spiritual inspiration to me since we married in 1979. And as this calling on my life grew, so did her desire to encourage me onward. Laura has encouraged my ministry to men pursuits since our days at Northside Methodist Church in Atlanta, Georgia. My wife has also been a ministry catalyst for me, as in 2010, when she agreed to follow in my 2009 Holy Land pilgrimage footsteps for her pilgrimage travels to the Holy Land. While in Jerusalem with Laura in 2010, my men's pilgrimage initiative, Behold the Man, emerged. If she had not said yes to that trip, I am not sure Behold the Man would have been born. Together, our main ministry focus, two by two, for 31 years has been our four sons, to whom this book is dedicated. We have also been especially blessed to have our niece, Olivia, with us since her freshman year in high school.

In Genesis 12, when God calls Abram (Abraham) to "go", he goes! In 1995, I was faced with a crisis in confidence with my call to ministry. I had discerned that God had called me to lay ministry and not ordination, but beyond that

I was unsure how to proceed. In confiding in my brother, David, about this crisis, he cleared the air immediately. He said, "Go. Pursue ministry to men; it is *you!*" His confidence in me was infectious. I took his wise advice and have never looked back.

Beginning with this acknowledgement, it should be obvious that my ministry has always been a partnership. The Holy Spirit has always led the way for me and kindled a fire in me to reach men. And this fire has grown stronger every year.

I am indebted to the partnerships with the following bishops that have led the way to significant advancement: Rt. Rev. Jack Iker, Rt. Rev. Rogers Harris, Rt. Rev. Dabney Smith, Rt. Rev. Edward Salmon Jr. and the former bishop John Lipscomb.

Those partnerships were joined with others, over 30 years, with key clergy and pastors including: Father Michael Durning, Pastor Bill Floyd, Father Jim Hedman, Father Eric Hillegas, Pastor Sharon Lewis, Pastor Kelvin Lumpkin, Father Chuck Mann, Father Rick Marsden, Father Andrew Mayes, Father Peter Moore, Father Fred Robinson, Father Doug Schart, Father Jerry Smith, Dr. Hayes Wicker, Pastor Brian Yost.

I want to call from this distinguished group one man in particular, Father Fred Robinson, who arrived at my church in 1994 as our rector. He has been my spiritual mentor and my number one men's ministry champion. He believed in this ministry initiative immediately and has given me constant support, direction, friendship and encouragement all these years. Thank you, Father Fred.

A priest and friend, Father Gary Wilde, stepped forward to assist me on this book with amazing conviction, experience and passion. Partnering with him on this project brought a dream to reality.

I literally could list hundreds of men I want to thank on this page. My men's ministry efforts have been a true brotherly partnership as God and I have partnered with every man with whom I have come into contact for the last 30 years! I can only say thank you, thank you from the bottom of my heart for standing with me, walking with me down this path and saying yes when I came to you instead of running the other way:

Edward Bermudez, Rick Blackmore, George Bloodworth, Dennis Bontrager, Scott Brewer, Bill Brush, Bart Cox, Tom Crook, Frank Dieckman, Paul Downer, Phil Downer, David Dusek, Mike Forbes, Tramm Hudson, David Hunihan, Don Ingle, Jeff Kern, Bob Kimes, Tommy Klein, Ray Lanier, John Lawrence, Hunter Leake, John Maxwell, Jack McClure, John McCoy, Clyde McDaniel, Todd Menke, Scott Merritt, Chuck Miller, Pete Mogavero, Richard Moore, Andy Morse, Todd Morton, John Napolitano, Bill Rethorst, Tom Riley, Allan Rogers, Howard Roshaven, Peter Rothermel, Dale Schlafer, Terry Simes, Doug Spangler, Carl Stockton, Billy Tullos, Tony Veldkamp, Dale Volrath, Brian Yost, Rob Zetterberg.

My sincere thanks to the amazing staff of many churches, especially Church of the Redeemer. I also owe a deep debt of gratitude to Father Fred Robinson and my wife, Laura, for their meticulous editing of my manuscript. And last, but by no means least, I want to thank, with great and heartfelt appreciation, my two longtime, former personal assistants, Helen Zubrinsky and Dede Smally.

Appendix A

Description of A Journey in Disciple Making and Recommended Resources

What we want men to find in our local congregations:

"Joining Christ in transforming the world is the adventure their hearts have always longed for."

—**Pat Morley**[1]

Your passion is ignited, your team is in place and you understand the challenge of men and the church. Furthermore, the model is almost in place to replace the undifferentiated priorities and activities, to remove the "default mode" for men, such as going to church when your wife shames you into it or being an usher or maybe serving on the finance committee and thinking that is involvement enough. Instead of these defaults, you are ready for all-inclusive ministry to men in your church. You are focused on intentional friendships and personal invitation. You've asked God to make you approachable in personality and infectiously inviting in action. Your church is taking on a new, vibrant look and feel.

Here's where the key question arises in your mind as you've gotten inspired about ministry to men: **What, exactly, is the Christian Formation** *content?* I simply recommend Jesus's model in the 21st century: disciple making. A JOURNEY IN DISCIPLE MAKING (AJDM) is a three to five-year comprehensive disciple-making process to "give men what they need in the context of what they want."

THE JOURNEY PROCESS
FOR THE LOCAL CHURCH

Worship
Engaging in worship with a biblical message allows men to experience an environment where a growing, intimate relationship with God is the primary concern.

"No Man Left Behind"
A man can't take that first step in the journey without a men's ministry infrastructure in place in his congregation. We rely on Pat Morley's model in *No Man Left Behind* to initiate and establish an effective ministry to men in the local church.

CONNECT

Entry Points: steak dinners, sports-related outings and other opportunities to make an initial effort by personal invitation to draw men into your church.

Bible Study: Weekly men's ministry fellowship opportunities to gather for study and prayer.

<u>COMMIT</u>

Accountability Groups: Weekly small-group meetings for accountability, encouragement and challenge to reach their potential as men of God.

Great Dads: Enhance your commitment and ability to be a godly father and mentor. This biblically based, four-hour workshop from Great Dads National Ministry will encourage and equip fathers to be more intentional about parenting their children. Great Dads seminars are for all men desiring to enhance their abilities in fathering.

Raising a Modern-day Knight: Six sessions for fathers to discover how to connect with their sons, understand issues in effective and strategic parenting and learn how to lead their sons into authentic manhood.

Seeking Him: This is a 12-week experience in personal, spiritual revival. The study was inspired by Psalm 69:32: "You who seek God, let your hearts revive." Each interactive lesson features five days of individual study followed by a group discussion section. Participants are renewed and revitalized as they explore topics including honesty, humility, repentance, grace, obedience and others. This is an ideal small-group, user-friendly program.

Men's Fraternity: This is a manhood series developed by the Rev. Robert Lewis, which includes the following.

1. **Quest for Authentic Manhood:** 24 sessions on man's core identity; basic manhood issues.
2. **Winning at Work and Home:** 16 sessions on engaging in your work; new way to relate to a woman.
3. **The Great Adventure:** 20 sessions on understanding the masculine identity and pursuing an authentic biblical manhood.

REACH

Explore: Created by Robert Lewis, author of the best-selling Men's Fraternity series. This five-week DVD training series will help men develop confidence and discover practical know-how for sharing their faith.

One 2 Won: Employing a basic training manual written by Joe White, *One 2 Won Cross-training* is a 24-week, two-man, team-equipping process that empowers men to become disciple makers for a lifetime.

LEAD

The Truth Project: A DVD-based small group curriculum, these 12 one-hour lessons are taught by Dr. Del Tackett. This study is a starting point for looking at life from a biblical perspective, with an emphasis on apologetics. Each lesson discusses in great detail the relevance and importance of living the Christian worldview in daily life.

Christian Leadership Concepts: All men find themselves in some kind of leadership role and most men feel unprepared to provide that leadership. Responsibilities at home, church, in business, or in community require men to be leaders. CLC is a two-year, small-group curriculum based on sound biblical principles and designed to equip men for leadership in every area of their lives. The program is designed for two hours per week for a total of 104 weeks.

Emerging Programs: Men and the Church is continuously researching and providing new programs to assist congregations on the journey in disciple making. See our website at www.menandthechurch.com

Behold the Man—Men's Pilgrimage to the Holy Land: By experiencing Jesus's earthly place and life, men grow in their understanding of who Jesus is and continues to be. It's designed for 12 men and 10 days.

STORY FROM THE MISSION FIELD

Pete Mogavero

When Jay asked me to join him for a remarkable religious journey to Jerusalem, I leapt at the chance. My trip goals were to:

- Learn more about my Christian heritage from a historical perspective.
- Discover the roots of the Jewish heritage and people.

Throughout my life, I have marveled at religious groups annually going to their "Holy Land" for religious pilgrimage experiences. What a neat concept to blend your faith with the actual places and history where it all began. What would it feel like to be at the actual places where Jesus walked and lived? Were there still primitive, pristine and virtually untouched areas of the Holy Land? Would I feel closer to God there? In a very real sense, I set out on my journey with Jay to get a palpable feel for the roots of my Christian traditions and beliefs. In my wildest dreams, I wasn't prepared for the glorious history, the astonishing maze and smells of the Holy City, Jerusalem and the many surprises along the way.

After the flight into Tel Aviv, our band of 12 men took a bus ride to Jerusalem. We soon arrived at St. George's College in the middle of Jerusalem, but outside the walled city. We stayed in dorms for the 10-day visit and were pleasantly surprised by the wonderful food! I was shocked to discover that our guide and inspirational educator, Father Kamal Farrah, was *not Jewish*, but rather he was a cross between four distinct groups and heritages: Arab, Palestinian, Israeli and Christian. The notion that he could be both Arab and Christian was mind-boggling. But, the notion that he was also a Palestinian/Israeli Christian really threw me for a loop. As I began to understand him and seek out his beliefs and knowledge, I was awe-struck by the depth of his Christian understanding. Challenges and perplexing contradictory points between religions all began to settle in my mind when Father Kamal would say "Ah. . .but this is the *happy confusion* of Christianity."

We journeyed to many remarkable sites. I was particularly struck and touched by the Sea of Galilee and the Mount of Beatitudes. It was startling to visit the Sea of Galilee with its untouched land and shoreline, just as it was when Jesus was alive. I marveled at the fact that this pristine lake didn't have huge mansions, condominiums or skyscrapers built around it. Fresh water is very dear to any people who live in the desert. I was astonished that it remained a lake in the midst of the desert with virtually no development around it. . . it was incredible, pure, crystal clear and virtually unchanged.

Inside the marvelous walled city of Jerusalem, you are captivated by the street vendors, the smell of spices, merchants selling religious icons and Persian carpets — all begging one to "come in for some relaxing tea, my friend." You can easily get lost in the multi-racial crowds that flow like a river through the alley ways, shops, caves, hidden stairs and rooftop paths. History truly comes alive in Jerusalem. While we, as Americans, have modern architecture and massive corporate campuses, the Israelis have so much more in Jerusalem. They have 10,000 years of history to sift through. Every place you look, time and history are etched on the walls. How remarkable it is to see such depth of historic riches all preserved to this day.

My faith was strengthened by all I learned, the people I was exposed to, the experience of studying and praying with Christian brothers and the overwhelming sense of pride and friendship I had while interacting with both Israelis and Palestinians. Neither words nor pictures can capture the true beauty that exists in Jerusalem. Each holy site brought a special appreciation and a new depth to my Christian understanding.

Emerging Programs: **Men and the Church** is continuously researching and providing new programs to assist congregations on the journey in disciple making. See our website at www.menandthechurch.com

THE JOURNEY PROCESS
IN MOTION

Worship
⬇
Your Church (Disciples)
⬇
A Journey in Disciple Making (Mentored/Equipped)
⬇
Disciple Makers (Sent)
⬇

Discipling New Men of Faith/Transforming
Their Community

Welcoming Men to Your Church

Worship

Your Church (Disciples)
⬇
An Example:
Episcopal Church of the Redeemer, Sarasota, Florida

Men of Redeemer (MOR)

Purpose: "Encouraging men, through relationships, to seek Christ-centered living."

MOR uses A Journey in Disciple Making as the process to achieve this purpose.

Ministry process: *A Journey in Disciple Making* (AJDM) is a straightforward and strategic process that moves men (18 years and older) through the stages of spiritual growth and defines the Great Commission (Matthew 28:19, 20) in the form of a simple, disciple making process.

The process flows as follows:

Clarity: the ability of AJDM to be communicated and understood by our men.

Movement: the steps in the process that cause men to move to greater areas of commitment. Movement is how someone is handed off from one level of commitment to a greater level of commitment in order to avoid allowing men

261

to remain in the same place spiritually for years. Without movement, we are just running ministry programs.

Alignment: the arrangement of all MOR team members and Redeemer clergy around our simple AJDM process in order to avoid being cluttered, complex and misaligned.

Focus: the MOR commitment to abandon everything that falls outside the simple AJDM ministry process. A lack of focus leads to scattering, which steals attention and energy from our process.

Benefits of the AJDM process for Men of Redeemer:

Increased morale: Men understand where they are going.

Urgency: We have a big vision with the conviction of achieving it.

Spiritual growth: The process shows men where they are and where they need to go next.

Conversion: AJDM allows men to feel and act confidently and competently toward others as disciples of Jesus Christ.

Expectation: Men find a defined process with the expectation of progression.

Stewardship: All our energies are focused on what works.

Unity: All Men of Redeemer are committed to a common vision with the process in place to achieve the vision.

Program development: We add only program options that build on our process and add to spiritual transformation. We avoid non-value-adding programs.

Recommended books

Date Your Wife, by Justin Buzzard

Eternal Impact: Investing in the Lives of Men,
by Phil Downer

Jesus Christ, Disciplemaker, by Bill Hull

No Man Left Behind, by Pat Morley

Raising a Modern-day Knight, by Robert Lewis

Raising a Modern-Day Princess, by Pam Farrel
and Doreen Hanna

Strong Fathers, Strong Daughters, by Meg Meeker

The Way of the Lord: Christian Pilgrimage Today,
by Tom Wright

Why Men Hate Going to Church,
by David Murrow

Websites Of Interest

Christian Leadership Concepts
www.christianleadershipconcepts.org

Eternal Impact
www.dnaministries.org

Great Dads
www.greatdads.org

Men's Fraternity
www.mensfraternity.com

Men and the Church
www.menandthechurch.com

Raising a Modern-day Knight
www.mdk.com

Why Men Hate Going to Church
www.churchformen.com

No Man Left Behind
www.maninthemirror.org

Appendix B

Pastor's Challenges and Concerns

W hat are the challenges and concerns of pastors related to the "launch" of a ministry to men in the local congregation? Here are some of the issues raised with me over the years and how I tend to respond.

Pastor: "People will say I'm giving all my time to the men. What about the women, youth, the sick, shut-ins and all the other ministries I need to oversee?"

Response: The pastor is a generalist, by necessity of course. But really, any pastor must become engaged in these two vital efforts: *personal discipling* (see the chapters 8 and 9) and *leadership team development.* These won't take away from any other ministry and, in fact, were a central key for Jesus! Our Lord's prime focus was three men, John, Peter and James, as well as the other nine apostles—all men! You may find a woman in your church who can develop discipleship among the women. If you are a woman pastor or priest, find a key male leader for your men, and help with his training.

Pastor: "I just don't have the time for one more ministry program."

Response: It's true that most pastors are stressed for time. For many, 12 to 14-hour days aren't unusual. But men's ministry isn't a program. It's a transformational environment that pervades a church, bringing vitality to every area of its common life. It does require having a layman as a champion and also a team to lead the ministry. Offer to help with delegating these tasks.

Pastor: "Isn't this all quite anti-woman?"

Response: No way! This is a particular emphasis because of the plight of male absenteeism in the local church. It in no way seeks to denigrate or ignore the exemplary Christian servanthood of women in the church. But it is crucial that we bring gender balance back into the life of our local congregations. Also, realize that key men's leaders pay much attention to women and their influence for Christ. See, for example, David Murrow's online presence directed to women: http://churchformen.com/women-start-here-2/

Pastor: "Men just don't like church."

Response: Actually, the deeper issue is most men don't know what the *purpose* of church is. When we ask something of them—like getting involved in carrying out the Great Commission—they begin to like and even come to thrive on church!

Pastor: "My congregation is too old, filled with retired people."

Response: Have you checked out the biblical concept of spiritual parenting? It is the duty of the elderly in society — and particularly the "elders" in a church congregation—to mentor the youth. Younger people, many now products of broken families, long for the attention of an older man to spend time with them and show them what it means to grow into adulthood. Developmental psychologists tell us that the main task of older adulthood is to convey wisdom to the coming generation. Older guys, your work is cut out for you, until you hit the grave!

Pastor: "Our church is too small."

Response: We will start with just one disciple. Pray and God will send him. The rest is pure multiplication (2 Timothy 2:2).

Pastor: "There's not really a need for it in our church."

Response: I go back to Pat Morley's weighty statement: "If you don't reach the men, within 30 years, you won't have a church."

Notes

Preface

1   David James, *What are they saying about Masculine Spirituality (Mahwah, NJ, Paulist Press, 1996),5.*

2   John Gray, *Men Are from Mars, Women Are from Venus* (San Francisco: Harper Paperbacks, 2004).

3   Steve Sonderman, *How to Build a Life-Changing Men's Ministry (Minneapolic, Bethany House Publishers, 1996),13-20.*

4   "Myths About Worshippers and Congregations: Results from the U.S. Congregational Life Survey," 1998, 2002, 2006-2007. www.uscongregations. org/myths.htm

5   Merriam-Webster, "benign neglect," http://www. merriam-webster.com/ dictionary/benign%20neglect

6   U.S. Congregational Life Survey, 1998, 2002,2006-2007.

7   The Episcopal Church, http://www.episcopalchurch. org/sites/default/files/downloads/domestic_fast_ facts_trends_2007-2011.pdf

Chapter 1: Where Are the Men?

1   David Murrow's website is a great source for statistics on men and the church. For these six items I

list, in this order, David Murrow, in *Why Men Hate Going to Church*, supplies these sources:

- "U.S. Congregational Life Survey – Key Findings," 29 October 2003, <www.uscongregations.org/key.htm>.
- This statistic comes from Barna's figures on male/female worship attendance, overlayed upon the Census 2000 numbers for adult men and women in the U.S. population.
- I came up with this figure by taking the U.S. Census 2000 numbers for total married adults and overlaying Barna Research's year 2000 percentages of male vs. female attendance at weekly worship services. The figures suggest at least 24.5 million married women attend church on a given weekend, but only 19 million married men attend. That's 5.5 million more women, or 22.5%. The actual number may be even higher, because married people attend church in much greater numbers than singles.
- "LifeWay Research Uncovers Reasons 18 to 22 Year Olds Drop Out of Church," PowerPoint presentation accompanying study, available at the LifeWay website, http://www.lifeway.com/lwc/article_main_page/0,1703,A=165949&M=200906,00.html (accessed 12 September 2007).
- Barna Research Group, "Women are the Backbone of Christian Congregations in America," www.barna.org, March 6, 2000.
- Based on a show of hands at the National Coalition of Men's Ministries meeting in 2005. The consensus in the room among hundreds of men's ministry experts was that less than 10 percent of congregations had any ongoing ministry to men. Compare this to the 110 percent of churches that offer women's and children's ministries.

Chapter 2: Who Are These Guys Today?

1 Collin Hansen, "Wanted, Young Men in the Church: Delayed Marriage Forecasts an Impending Crisis," *Christianity Today Online,* March 7, 2008. This article located at: http://www.christianitytoday.com/ct/2008/marchweb-only/110-52.0.html

2 From an anonymous pastor, at the time of this writing, quoted at: http://pastorhogg.wordpress.com/

3 These statistics according to Barna research reported in the book *You Lost Me,* by David Kinnaman (Grand Rapids: Baker, 2011), 46-47. Kinnaman cites Robert Wuthnow's stats, in footnote 5 of Wuthnow's book, *After the Baby Boomers: How Twenty-and Thirty-Somethings Are Shaping the Future of American Religion* (Princeton, NJ: Princeton University Press, 2007), 11.

4 David Kinnaman, *You Lost Me,* (Grand Rapids, MI: Baker Books (October 1, 2011), 47ff.

5 David Brooks, "The Odyssey Years," *New York Times,* October 9, 2007. The article is online at: http://www.nytimes.com/2007/10/09/opinion/09brooks.html

6 Collin Hanson ("Wanted, Young Men in the Church") quotes these statistics from Kay S. Hymowitz's article, "Child-Man in the Promised Land" (*City Journal,* Winter 2008, vol. 18, no. 1).

7 This quote by Smith and Denton taken from the dust jacket of the book, *Almost Christian: What the Faith of Our Teenagers Is Telling the American Church* (New York: Oxford University Press, 2012), by Kenda Creasy Dean.

8 The USA Today article by Cathy Lynn Grossman was published on April 27, 2010. It can be found online here:

http://usatoday30.usatoday.com/news/religion/2010-
04-27-1Amillfaith27_ST_N.htm
(Note: The Comments section is no longer available
at the online site.)
9   Kenda Creasy Dean, *Almost Christian: What the
Faith of Our Teenagers Is Telling the American
Church* (New York: Oxford University Press, 2012),
dust jacket.
10   C.S. Lewis, *God in the Dock* (Grand Rapids, MI:
Wm B. Eerdmans, 1972), 101.
11   Thomas Rainer, president and CEO, LifeWay Christian
Resources at: http://blogs.lifeway.com/cgi-bin/mt/
mt-search.cgi?blog_id=8&tag=research&limit=20

Chapter 3: What's Their Cultural Challenge?

1   Hansen, "Wanted, Young Men in the Church."
2   See the info on this sitcom at Parents Television
Council, http://www.parentstv.org/ptc/shows/main.
asp?shwid=1771
3   Fr. Richard Kew quotes professor Stephen Bergman
here. I am greatly indebted to my friend Richard
Kew (Anglican priest serving as Development
Director for Ridley College, Cambridge), for many
of the ideas on postmodern culture summarized in
this chapter. He gave a marvelous talk on the topic at
the Episcopal Diocese of Southwest Florida's men's
conference in the early 2000s.
4   Chart material adapted (with my thanks) from
information found on the Pastor Michael Hogg
website, located here: http://pastorhogg.wordpress.
com/2012/08/20/the-american-church-in-the-future/
5   Barbara Engler, *Personality Theories* (Beverly, MA:
Wadsworth Publishing, 8th ed., 2008), 157.

6   Robert Lewis, "The Quest for Authentic Manhood" DVD (Nashville: LifeWay, 2004). Order the series here: http://mensfraternity.com/products

7   See Lewis's book, *Raising the Modern Day Knight*, (Carol Stream, IL: Tyndale House, 2007), for a full description of these four qualities of authentic manhood.

Chapter 4: What's in Their Minds?

1   Men's Health, quoted in *Parade Magazine*, December 29, 1991, 5.

2   Ronald Rohlheiser, *The Holy Longing: The Search for a Christian Spirituality* (Colorado Springs: Image Books, 2014).

3   John Bradshaw, *Healing the Shame that Binds You* (Deerfield Beach, FL: Health Communications, Inc., 1988), n.p.

Chapter 5: Are You Ready to Befriend the Unchurched Man?

1   Billy Graham, quoted in Ray Comfort, *How to Live Forever Without Being Religious* (Alachua, FL: Bridge-Logos Publishers, 2006), 60.

2   Quotes by Badajoz soldiers found in online chapters of the book, *The Real War of 1812: The Storming of Badajoz* at http://www.twcenter.net/forums

3   Robert Putnam, *Bowling Alone: The Collapse and Revival of American Community* (New York: Touchstone Books, 2001).

4   Garrison Keillor, *The Book of Guys* (New York: Viking Press, 1993), 20.

5   The quote by B.F. Westcott, Anglican bishop (January 12, 1825 to July 27, 1901) is found online at: http://izquotes.com/quote/196390

6   Earl Roe, ed., *Dream Big: The Henrietta Mears Story* (Ventura, CA: Regal Books, 1990), 18.

7   Alfred C. Krass, "What the Mainline Denominations Are Doing in Evangelism," *Christian Century,* May 2, 1979, 490, quoting Masumi Toyotome.

8   A. W. Tozer, *The Pursuit of God* (Camp Hill, PA: Wingspread Publishers, 2006), 11.

9   Gary Smalley and John Trent, *The Blessing* (Nashville: Thomas Nelson Publishers, 1986). To order this book, call: 800-834-7828.

10 Putnam, *Bowling Alone,* 58.

11 Alan W. Jones, *Soul Making: The Desert Way of Spirituality* (San Francisco: Harper & Row, Publishers, 1985), 15.

12 *The State of the Church & Family Report: How Parents Are Rethinking Their Connections with Churches,* 2010 Annual Report © 2010 Orange, a division of the reTHINK Group.

13 Peter Haas, *Pharisectomy: How to Joyfully Remove Your Inner Pharisee and other Religiously Transmitted Diseases* (Springfield, MO: Influence Resources, 2012), 33.

Chapter 6: Can You Man Up Your Church?

1   Keilor, *The Book of Guys,* 18.

2   *The State of the Church & Family Report,* 2010 Annual Report.

3   David Murrow, *Why Men Hate Going to Church* (Nashville: Thomas Nelson, 2001), 58.

4   Robert Penn Warren, in his essay, "Why Do We Read Fiction?" published in *The Saturday Evening Post,*

July/August 1986. It can be viewed online here: http://rpwcirclesite.files.wordpress.com/2013/01/ why_fiction_by_rpw.pdf

5   Michael Slaughter, *UnLearning Church* (Nashville: Abingdon Press, 2008), 43.

6   Peter Haas, *Pharisectomy*, 116.

7   Dan Erickson and Dan Schaffer, "Modern Man in Contemporary Culture," in *Effective Men's Ministry*, ed. Phil Downer (Grand Rapids: Zondervan & National Coalition of Men's Ministries, 2001), 20.

Chapter 7: Do You Have a Structure in Place?

1   Pat Morley, *No Man Left Behind: How to Build and Sustain a Thriving Disciple-Making Ministry for Every Man in Your Church* (Chicago, IL: Moody Publishers, 2006), 20.

2   Steve Sonderman, "Organizing Your Men's Ministry," in *Effective Men's Ministry*, 79.

3   See C. Kirk Hadaway, "FACTs on Growth: A new look at the dynamics of growth and decline in American congregations based on the Faith Communities Today 2005 national survey of Congregations." Hartford Institute for Religion Research, found online at: http://hirr.hartsem.edu

4   Morley, *No Man Left Behind*, 60.

5   Ibid., 90.

6   Ibid., 209.

Chapter 8: Have You Heard the Call to Discipling?

1   Bill Hull, *Jesus Christ, Disciplemaker* (Grand Rapids: Baker, 2004), 52.

2   These statistics given in the C. S. Lewis Institute article title, "Sparking a Discipleship Movement in

America and Beyond," 2011, 2, found on the web at: http://www.cslewisinstitute.org/webfm_send/210 The CS Lewis Institute, 8001 Braddock Road, Suite 301 Springfield, VA 22703-914-5602

3   John Stott, quoted in "Sparking a Discipleship Movement," 2.

4   Joe Maxwell, "Men Are Back," The National Coalition of Men's Ministries, http://www.strang.com/nm/online/nm900/nm9001.htm

5   Gordon Dalbey, quoted in "Men are Back."

6   Hull, *Jesus Christ, Disciplemaker*, 13.

7   Phil Downer, "Becoming a Spiritual Parent," in *Effective Men's Ministry*, 177.

8   Gary Wilde, "Lone Rangers—or Disciples?" *The Moultrie Observer*, March 5, 2009. Used with permission of the author.

Chapter 9: Do You Know the Nuts and Bolts of Disciple Making?

1   Steve Sonderman, *Mobilizing Men for One-on-One Ministry: The Transforming Power of Authentic Friendship and Discipleship* (Grand Rapids, MI: Bethany House Publishers, 2010), 79.

2   Morley, *No Man Left Behind*, 166.

3   Pastor Steve Scarrow, Friendship Alliance Church, Moultrie, Georgia.

4   David R. Hopkins, *Multiplying Disciples: Increasing the Kingdom of God One Person at a Time* (Franklin Springs, GA: LifeSprings Resources, 2009), 142.

5   Hopkins, *Multiplying Disciples*, 140.

6   Phil Downer, "Becoming a Spiritual Parent," in *Effective Men's Ministry*, 179.

7   Barna is summarized in this statement found in Bill Hull, *Jesus Christ, Disciplemaker* (Grand Rapids:

Baker, 2004), p. 15. Hull refers in his footnote to George Barna, *Growing True Disciples* (Colorado Springs: Waterbrook Press, 2001), 54-55.

Chapter 10: Can You Pastor Their Hearts?

1   McCartney's quote from 2001 is cited in Maxwell, "Men Are Back."
2   This section on the father wound adapts and draws heavily upon my editor Gary Wilde's personal father-wound story, which appeared in the book *Receiving Love,* by Joseph Biuso, Brian Newman and Gary Wilde (Colorado Springs: Chariot Victor Books, 1996).

   Wilde's story also appears in *Just Add Jesus,* by James Stuart Bell and Gary Wilde (Avon, MA: Adams Media Corporation, 2006). It is used here with permission of the author, Gary Wilde, who is my friend and colleague in men's ministry in the Episcopal Diocese of Southwest Florida. Ordering information:
   Receiving Love—Call 1.800.743.2514
   Just Add Jesus—Call 1.800.872.5627
3   Daniel Moore, *Warrior Wisdom* (Philadelphia: Running Press, 1993), 12.
4   Tom Fortson, "Top Ten Things Promise Keepers Has Learned about Men," *Christian Counseling Today,* 2006 Vol. 14, No. 1, 36-39.
5   Kevin McClone, "Male Intimacy: Men's Longing for Intimacy and Connections," *Touchstone*, Winter 2001, 5-7.
6   C. S. Lewis, *The Problem of Pain* (New York: HarperCollins, 2001), 94.

Chapter 11: Blessed through His Chosen Denomination

1   Gary Thomas, *Sacred Pathways: Discover Your Soul's Path to God* (Grand Rapids, MI: Zondervan, 1996).
2   Several fine studies and books have spoken of these "kinds" as spiritual temperaments, or God languages, or forms of piety. I'd like to explore this with you because, as a leader of men, you'll want to be aware of what kinds of spiritual temperaments you'll be encountering in your ministry. I use as my key sources three excellent books: *The Sacred Pathways* (Grand Rapids: Zondervan, 2010), by Gary Thomas; *What's Your God Language?* (Carol Stream, IL: Tyndale, 2007) by Myra Perrine; and *Uncommon Prayer* (Columbus, MI: Genesis Press, 1987), by Kenneth Swanson. I highly recommend each of these for your own men's ministry bookshelf. Ordering info:
     Sacred Pathways, Zondervan —800-226-1122
     What's Your God Language? Tyndale House —800-323-9400
     Uncommon Prayer, Genesis Press—888-463-4461
3   Perrine, *What's Your God Language,* 13. Perrine's inventory is especially helpful.
4   "Don" is a real person but with details of name and life situation disguised.
5   See Thomas, *The Sacred Pathways,* and Perrine, *What's Your God Language?*
6   Thomas, *Sacred Pathways,* 20-21.
7   The Heritage Foundation, "Why Religion Matters: The Impact of Religious Practice on Social Stability," The Heritage Foundation Backgrounder 1064, January 25, 1996, <www.heritage.org>.
8   Ibid.

9 Penny Edgell (Becker) and Heather Hofmeister, "Work, Family and Religious Involvement for Men and Women," Hartford Institute for Religion Research, <http://hirr.hartsem.edu>.

10 Christian Smith and Phillip Kim, "Religious Youth Are More Likely to Have Positive Relationships with Their Fathers," University of North Carolina at Chapel Hill, July 12, 2002, findings based on the National Longitudinal Survey of Youth (1997).

11 C. Kirk Hadaway, "FACTs on Growth: A new look at the dynamics of growth and decline in American congregations based on the Faith Communities Today 2005 national survey of Congregations." Hartford Institute for Religion Research, http://hirr.hartsem.edu.

12 Perrine, *What's Your God Language?* 115-17.

13 Swanson, *Uncommon Prayer,* 58.

14 Ibid., 64.

15 Ibid., 71.

16 Ibid., 76.

17 Thomas, *Sacred Pathways,* 239.

Chapter 12: Blessed in His Journey Inward: Coming Home

1 Alan Jones, *Soul Making: The Desert Way of Spirituality* (San Francisco: HarperOne, 1989), 145.

2 Philip Yancey, *Prayer: Does It Make Any Difference?* (Grand Rapids: Zondervan, 2010), 42, 44.

3 Gerald May, quoted in *Receiving Love,* by Joseph Biuso and Brian Newman (Colorado Springs: Chariot Victor Books, 1996), p. 113.

4 Gary Wilde, *Integrity: Character Counts* (Wheaton, IL: Victor Books/SP Publications, 1996), 38-39.

5 Jones, *Soul Making,* 155.

Chapter 13: Blessed in His Journey Godward: Surrender

1   V. Raymond Edmund, former president of Wheaton College, quoted in Gary Wilde, *Spirituality: Loved by God* (Wheaton, IL: Victor Books/SP Publications, 1996), n.p.
2   C.S. Lewis, *Mere Christianity* (New York, NY: Simon & Schuster, 1996), chap. 27.
3   See www.disciplehouse.net.
4   Oswald Chambers, *My Utmost for His Highest* (Grand Rapids, MI: Discovery House Publishers, 1992), un-numbered page entry for July 20th.

Chapter 14: Blessed in His Journey Outward: Belonging and Service

1   Dean, *Almost Christian*, 65.
2   This chart adapted from an article in *New Man Magazine*, by George Barna, titled "The Battle for the Hearts of Men," *New Man* 4, no. 1 (1997): 40-44.
3   This section draws from the introduction to the *Encouragers for Men* book series by Gary Wilde (Wheaton, IL: Victor) and is used by permission of the author.
4   Henri Nouwen, *In the Name of Jesus: Reflections on Christian Leadership* (New York: Crossroad Publishing, 2001), 47-48.

Appendix A: Description of A Journey in Disciple Making and Recommended Resources

1   Morley, *No Man Left Behind*, 153.

CHURCH LEADERS AND EMERGING LEADERS:

This book is the core curriculum for my equipping conference to welcome men back to your church. The conference is specifically designed for:

SEMINARIES
DENOMINATIONAL LEADERS
REGIONAL CHURCH CONFERENCES

It is also intended to foster collaborative research and study in the field of masculine spirituality in the 21st century.

FOR FURTHER INFORMATION CONTACT

jaycrouse@aol.com | menandthechurch.com

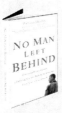

CPSIA information can be obtained at www.ICGtesting.com
Printed in the USA
LVOW13s1822101013

356246LV00003B/3/P